Lea Maria Spahn ed.

Walking as Embodied Worldmaking
Bodies, Borders, Knowledgescapes

Content

8   Contributors

15   Lea Maria Spahn
       Introduction: Bodies – Borders – Knowledgescapes

1st Part
Posthuman Imaginations – Walking in a More-than-human World

30   inka°witz
       Passers-by*

36   Mariele Weber
       "Another Gaze" – Seeing the World from the Perspective of a Plant

48   Lea Maria Spahn
       Posthuman Bodyscapes – Walking in the Czech-German Borderland

60   Astrid Lembcke-Thiel
       Footnotes

2nd Part
Walking in the (Performative) Arts

82   Antonin Brinda
       East by Northeast: (Dis)Obedient Walking, (Dis)Obedient Riding

104   ANa Anaa
       Bodies of Transit

116   Hana Magdoňová
       39 Days in the Plain

128   Otto Kauppinen
       Walking and Physical Movement as a Vehicle of Immersion

3rd Part
Walking as Method(ology)

142   Shira Wachsmann
        The Moment Before – War Trauma, Embodiment, and the Re-Membering
        of Matter (and what matters)

152   Marie Kammler
        Strollology as a State of Mind An Aesthetic Approach and Intervention to
        Pedestrian Centred Urban Planning

164   Maja Maksimović, Darija Medić & Mirjana Utvić
        Notes in Public Space: Inscribing the Pavement, Annotating the City

4th Part
Situated Experiences while Walking

178   Dorothea Hamilton
        2,54 cm away from Flying – Or: Walking in the Skies as a Feminist

186   Susanne Nemmerz
        Long-Distance Hiking – Arriving. Lingering. Walking on.

196   Regula Pöhl & Daniela Villiger / Zündwerk
        Every Wednesday. Action 05–20

206   Eva Clara Tenzler
        Gehen – Ein Längsschnitt Walking – Dissecting
        (Walking as Physical Poetry)

Contributors

ANA ANAA (D/F) embraces bodies in transit, in trance. I position myself as a passeur, someone inviting and guiding into other realms deeply engaged in decolonial gestures. I continuously reformulate and elaborate languages reflecting on presences and presents. I intend to seek via immersive installations for futures cherishing multiple temporalities. I imagine L'entre deux mondes as a performative twilight. A realm challenging fiction as much as reality. My approach is polymorphic, ranging from writings that are edited and activated through performed lectures, to video montage, to ephemeral sculptures as well as to ceramics, to sound and light impregnating a place. My artistic research is about human and non-human coexistence in environments that tend to become more and more precarious. I generate an archive of entangled voices relating to alternative histories. I wish to create refuges and territories of/for care.

ANTONÍN BRINDA is a Czech artist based in Europe, works in the fields of performance/urban/walking/body art. He creates minimalist, conceptual, long durational works exploring areas such as urbanism, transportation infrastructure, political geography, or international mobility. To balance the serious topics, he also likes to present other types of performances that are more personal and humorous. He is a graduate from different fields of art and art theory. Apart from an artist, he is also an organizer/curator of various (performance) art events and festivals. Antonín would like to know, "How to make love with a city".
Homepage: antoninbrinda.com

ASTRID LEMBCKE-THIEL (Dipl.-Ing./M.A.) is a German freelance curator for artistic processes, creativity extremist and Punktum researcher. In addition to her work as a consultant for cultural education at the Hessian State Museum of Art and Nature, Wiesbaden, she is a lecturer, instructor in teacher and educator training courses and initiator of various projects and collaborations. A special focus of her work is the relationship between space, place, material and bodily communication.

DARIJA MEDIĆ is an artist, educator and cultural worker in academia and civil society, researching labyrinths of contemporary meaning making in cohabitation with algorithmic technology through an intersectional data feminist lens. She develops work in the context of media poetics, distributed cognition, materiality of interaction and politics of interface design through creating collective participatory processes for sensitizing points of digital mediation. She shows work independently and collectively on conferences, exhibitions and festivals, making connections between critical media art, human computer interaction and digital policy. She graduated from the New Media Art department at the Academy of Arts in Novi Sad in Serbia, Master Media Design and Communication master from the Piet Zwart Institute in Rotterdam in the Netherlands and is currently a PhD student at the Intermedia Art, Writing and Performance Program at the University of Colorado, Boulder in the USA. She is a member of the Association of Visual Artists of Vojvodina, visiting lecturer at the Faculty for Media and Communications in Belgrade and associate researcher with kuda.org.

When not highlining, DOROTHEA HAMILTON (D) holds a phD Human Geography at the Justus Liebig University of Gießen (2021) and since been a transhumant scientist working on short-term contracts at different universities (University of Marburg, University of Hagen and Catholic University in Lima (PUCP). She has 4 kids. Much of her life is about keeping the balance.
Instagram: @highlining_mom

EVA CLARA TENZLER (D) works as a process facilitator, consultant and author for civil society initiatives, artists and transformation in organizations, regional development processes. In her poetic writings she researches between phenomenological explorations and somatic experiences. She studied philosophy-arts-media at the University of Hildesheim specialized on phenomenology and transcultural philosophies.
evaclaratenzler.de

HANA MAGDOŇOVÁ (CZ, 1989) is a Performance art artist and researcher. The main field of her work is the bodily liminal experience, which is present in performative situations as well as transitional rituals. The methods of her work are based on the methods of the shamanic craft of bodily ecstasy or trance. She thinks about art more as a state of being that precedes the act in the material world and defines it as pre-media. The visual experience is always in the background at the expense of the physical experience (whether of one's own body during a performance or a collective one within participatory happenings). The resulting effort is to sensitize our senses and expand our experience to include mythological and posthumanist realities, which should merge into one in the context of deep ecology. Hana is currently researching these topics as part of her doctoral studies at the Faculty of Arts, Brno University of Technology, Czechia, and applies them to her other projects and collaborations: Agronauts* Collective and Realities Research Lab.

INKA°WITZ (D) is rooted in many places and cannot decide where to belong. For her, staying is a radical act. Her writing may be young, but her connection and love to words is old. The focus of her work is on the spoken word on stage. From 2014 to 2018, she studied acting at the University of Art in Graz. She works as an actress. She is looking for an open feminist view of the world that leaves gaps and opens up spaces. She plays, writes, teaches, invents, researches, is human, child of a mother, sibling of brothers and sisters, friend, lover, and fighter for utopias. Both in theater and in writing, she sees the opportunity to struggle for tenderness.

LEA MARIA SPAHN (D) is a feminist and phenomenological researcher interested in a posthumanist view on the social and the agency of all kinds of bodies. In her PhD, she addressed the aging body with an ethnographic approach and movement practice. Since 2021, she has worked at the intersection of art and education in movement as a lecturer for dance education and philosophies of movement at the Philipps University of Marburg where she focuses on aesthetic and performative research. Currently, she is also part of the EU-Horizon project "Transforming Education for Democracy through Aesthetic and Embodied Learning, Responsive Pedagogies and Democracy-as-becoming" (AECED). In her artistic work, she is interested in performative art in public spaces and participatory action for livable futures. She is a co-founder of the German-Czech Agronauts* Collective which works on aesthetic practices as politics of naturecultures.

MAJA MAKSIMOVIĆ (SRB) is an Assistant Professor at the Department of Pedagogy and Andragogy at the Faculty of Philosophy of the University of Belgrade. At the moment, she focuses her research practice on the entanglement of the educational, activist, and artistic, trying to incorporate the critical, embodied, spatial and imaginative into a repertoire of action. Previously, her research mainly centred on the critical discourse analysis of various concepts of adult education and learning (lifelong learning, quality of education, etc.), but also inquiry into the historical emergence of adult education policies in Serbia through postcolonial lenses. She is a part of ESREA steering committee and a co-convenor of the ESREA network Active Democratic Citizenship and Adult Learning. Maja is also a member of Škograd collective.

MIRJANA UTVIĆ is an architect, maker and urban explorer based in Belgrade, Serbia. She designs and crafts tools and spaces, with the intention to empower critical thinking and creativity within the local community, by triggering experimentation, play and co-creation. Her research and practice are developed through her work in the Schoolcity since 2016, Center for the Promotion of Science since 2015, School of Urban Practices since 2012 and the City Guerilla creative laboratory since 2011. She is the author of multiple temporary public and multimedia interactive objects, installations and exhibitions.

MARIELE WEBER (D) is a wild plant educator from Marburg and offers herbal excursions and plant workshops that provide a healing, edible or creative approach to wild plants. As an environmental educator and adventure and outdoor educator (M.A.), she sees herself as a mediator between people and the plant world, making the fascinating world of wild plants accessible to children and adults. On the road, her eyes follow the multifaceted green of different landscapes. She also works in political education and is an educational officer with a passion for a variety of educational approaches in terms of socio-ecological transformation and a future worth living.
bne-marburg.de/organisation/wildwachsend/

MARIE-SOPHIE KAMMLER (D) is an interim professor for Aesthetic Education in the Department of Social Work at Ludwigshafen University of Business and Society, with a background in product and systemic design. As a co-founder of Raamwerk Studio she works in the field of relational design and participatory urban interventions. Next to this she was part of the Education and Learning departments for exhibitions like documenta 13 and 14 in Kassel and Manifesta 12 in Palermo. Today, while teaching, she is responsible for the Social Innovation Lab, a project by HWG LU, that aims to converge the university and urban society, together facing societal challenges.

OTTO KAUPPINEN is a doctoral student at the Theatre Faculty of Janáček Academy of Music and Performing Arts in Brno (JAMU) where he finished his masters degree in theatre dramaturgy. He is interested in political art (especially theatre) and in his research, he explores the emergence of relational aesthetics in contemporary theatre and the consequent question of politicality of participation. He worked as a dramaturg for the socially engaged theatre group Divadlo Feste theatre in Brno and with the physical theatre group Divadlo Continuo Theatre in Malovice as a dramaturg and director. Since 2019 he has been part of Agronauts* Collective art group that facilitated international art symposium Crossing Borders and uses the surrounding environment as a focus point for artists from different fields to work together. The group organized an exhibition at FFA Gallery (Faculty of Fine Arts, Brno University of Technology) in April 2022. In 2022 Otto co-founded Divadlo Láska Theatre in Prague and has worked as a dramaturg there ever since. He is bilingual and has translated 17 contemporary Finnish theatre plays into Czech. For his translations, he has been awarded the Evald Schorm Prize for young talented Czech playwrights and translators.

SHANNON SULLIVAN is known for the percussive power of her interdisciplinary poetic performances. 2022 she was nominated for the European-wide poetry network Versopolis. Her poetry confronts the dark spaces of the personal and collective psyches with an intent on transformation. With a keen eye, she penetrates the interrelatedness of microcosm and macrocosm. The images in her work range from deeply personal to global as she careens through an almost dizzying kaleidoscope of emotional landscapes. Interweaving music and poetry is a passion of Sullivan's. Sound and rhythm provide the heartbeat which propels the listener towards metamorphosis. Her work has been shown in numerous festivals in Europe and beyond; her poems have been translated into German, French, Spanish, Armenian, Slovak, Macedonian, Dutch, and Italian. "THE DIFFERENCE BETWEEN F. & F.", a collaboration with the musicians Ali Hasan and Simon Schmidt, has now been recorded as her first full-length album.
shannonsullivan.de

SUSANNE NEMMERTZ *1969, organisational consultant and coach, architect, educator. Since 1997 long-distance hikes in the Pyrenees, Patagonia and the Alps. 2001–2004 Postgraduate studies in architecture at the Düsseldorf Art Academy. 2004–2005 Master Class Integration Visual Arts and Architecture at the Düsseldorf Academy of Arts. Since 2004 Member of the Commission for Pedagogical Anthropology, German Society for Educational Science. 2019–2022 Master's degree in Organisational Consulting, Coaching, Supervision at ZHAW Institute of Psychology. She has been working with spatial experiences in movement for 20 years. These experiences flow into her work and shape her perspective on people's perceptions and actions in their respective work and life situations. Susanne Nemmertz lives and works in Stetten, Switzerland.

SHIRA WACHSMANN is a multidisciplinary artist and researcher working across moving image, installation, collage, drawing, digital, and electronic arts. Her practice takes a poetic, sensuous form--often multi-threaded, non-linear, and collective--addressing contemporary issues such as human-interspecies-machinic co-evolution and war trauma. Her recently completed practice-led Ph.D., *Landscape, War Trauma, Explosion: Re-membering the Moment Before*, delves into the complexities of war trauma. Internationally exhibited, Wachsmann's contemporary artworks include a mix of technologies and materials; filming/printing, animation, text, AR development, alongside various forms of sonic intelligence (incorporating ultrasonic sound and other multi-modal data inputs). Together with Dr. John Wild, she is the co-founder of *Symbiotic Intelligence*—rethinking AI through mycelium. In 2022, Wachsmann co-founded (with Dr. Ameera Kawash) the groundbreaking *Orbital Bloom*, a sophisticated data-driven work that enables individual users to emotionally connect and impact their environmental spaces. Currently teaches digital storytelling on the *Digital Direction* programme, at the Royal College of Art, London UK. Wachsmann has participated as an invited artist and speaker worldwide, including most recently in the UK/EU, the Middle East, and the global South.

ZÜNDWERK: The artists' collective has been creating actions in public space since 2003. In their works, habits of perception are questioned and spaces for thought and action are opened up, which invite the recipients to interact. The focus is on perception and the formation of an aesthetic awareness. They work at the interface between social systems and art. Continuously they focus on the contemplation of their own collaboration. ZündWerk consists of Regula Pöhl and Daniela Villiger and received a sponsorship award from the Canton of St. Gallen in 2018.

REGULA PÖHL (CH) *1974 studied Art Education ZHdK, lecturer at the Institute for Cultural and Aesthetic Education at the University of Education St. Gallen, Master of Arts Cultural Education at Schools.

DANIELA VILLIGER (CH) *1975, studied Art Education ZHdK, custom shoemaker, vegetable gardener of the assoziative schwarzes schaf.

Lea Maria Spahn

Introduction: Bodies – Borders – Knowledgescapes

Walking is as much a cultural practice as it is an embodied worldmaking. As Rebecca Solnit writes, it is a way to get to know "the world through the body and the body through the world".[1] As simple as this may sound, the contributions of this book engage with walking as practice in very different ways and offer a spectral view on walking within (artistic) research. With a focus on walking as embodied worldmaking, the book emphasizes the entanglement of bodies and specific environments as relational and dynamic becoming.

But let's begin with the body: Holding this book in your hands has surely involved some movement, some steps, a walk. Each step is a shift of weight from one to the other side of the body, the lifting of one foot, stepping out, and that moment of falling into the ground while your other foot is already rolling off the ground. Rarely do we consciously tune this deeply into our walking. In everyday life walking is often a functional way of moving through space; 'it gets us *somewhere*'. Nevertheless, walking is whole-bodied movement necessitating rhythm, acts of finding balance, finely orchestrated moments of sensory impression and proprioception with its felt relations to gravity, space and situated somatic responses.

Walking is bound to the materiality of being a body where implicitly the conditions of movement arise from being *here*, having location. With a phenomenological perspective, the *here* refers to the lived body that is the foundation of any subjective experience. *Here* is not a position in relation to external coordinates, rather, it is the "the laying down of the first coordinates, the anchoring of the active body in an object, the situation of the body in the face of its tasks".[2] With the lived body as foundational experience, we are closely related to gravity and the sensation of having a ground; we are enabled to be in the world as body with our motoric development starting in the womb already, born into a world in which any bodily practice is embedded in and part of social situations. Thus, the *here* is a reference point of the book both for situated analyses of walking as embodied practice and as a metaphor for the phenomenological conception of bodies as 'being towards the world'.[3] Maurice Merleau-Ponty, as a central figure in that regard, highlights bodies as a fundamental condition of our experience, incorporating the political, cultural, historical (sensory) orders they are embedded in – and an active participant in situations based on our embodied habits and knowledge. The here delineates corporeal situatedness in two senses: as an existential condition of 'being in the world' and as 'politics of location' which may also serve as a source of political engagement by subverting normative orders or 'going astray' – and thereby creating (other) ways of being in the world, an idea that this book rests upon.

[1] Solnit, R. (2000). *Wanderlust: A history of walking.* New York: Penguin Books Ltd., p. 29

[2] Young, I. M. (2005). *On female body experience: "Throwing like a girl" and other essays.* Oxford: Oxford University Press, p. 150

[3] Merleau-Ponty, M. (2002 [1966]). *Phenomenology of perception* (C. Smith, Trans.). London: Routledge

In that way, walking is a bodily practice of moving in and through a world – with the paths chosen according to (social) needs, desires, tasks, and always in relation to spatial specificities. And in turn, walking is also performatively co-constituting that world. However, it should be emphasized that any analysis of walking has to stay sensitive to differently-abled bodies and their ways of moving around.[4] But could an inclusive perspective even reach beyond an anthropocentric focus on human movement and also consider walking within a more-than-human world? These perspectives outline a first grounding for this collection.

[4] Every mover has a quite unique way of walking but also 'going on a walk' is just as possible with walking aids or in a wheelchair.

Why walking?

"Walking itself is the intentional act closest to the unwilled rhythms of the body, to breathing and the beating of the heart. It strikes a delicate balance between working and idling, being and doing. It is a bodily labor that produces nothing but thoughts, experiences, arrivals."[5]

This book emerged from noticing my body as walking body, from noticing the ubiquity of moving bodies, and from noticing the world through walking. Moving bodies are responsive bodies; through moments of registering, perceiving, listening, and feeling we are perceptive agents in two ways: Bodies *are experienced* as material and subjectively lived organism but as a responsive sensorium. And as bodies we *experience* our surroundings through continuously and swiftly changing sensory impressions. This twofold presence of our bodies is especially reflected on by researchers in phenomenology and sociology of the body[6]: as experienced body with felt needs, sensations, and a physiological uniqueness and as experiencing bodily subject of and toward the world. Both aspects are embedded in the biographical journeys of subjects as well as cultural and societal practices of moving, caring, treating, and sensing the body. Therefore, walking can be applied as an embodied method(ology) for doing social research sensitive to sensate and kinaesthetic attributes that connect lived experiences, memories, imaginations, communities, and identities.[7]

[5] Solnit, 2000, p. 5

[6] Crossley, N. (1995). Merleau-Ponty, the elusive body and carnal sociology. *Body & Society, 1*(1), 43–63

[7] O'Neill, M., & Roberts, B. (2020). *Walking methods: Research on the move.* London: Routledge; Springgay, S., & Truman, S. E. (Eds.). (2019). *Walking methodologies in a more-than-human world* (1st ed.). London: Routledge

WALKING: "A VITAL ART OF INQUIRY"[8]: BRIDGING WALKING ART AND METHODOLOGICAL ACCOUNTS

This becomes apparent in walking art[9] – may it be Richard Long's "A line made by walking" (1967) in which he created a temporal line in a landscape by walking back and forth on grass, the durational performance "The Lovers" by Marina Abramović and Ulay walking toward each other on the Chinese Wall in 1988, the renown walk works by Hamish Fulton or contemporary artists like Kuba Khademi who walked through public space in Afghanistan wearing a steel torso of female body in her performance "Armor". However, walking has also entered the social sciences and the manifold practices of contemporary art education as methodology.

[8] Lasczik, A., Rousell, D., & Cutter-Mackenzie-Knowles, A. (2023). Walking as a critical art of inquiry. In A. Lasczik, D. Rousell, & A. Cutter-Mackenzie-Knowles (Eds.), Walking as critical inquiry. Cham: Springer, 1–12

[9] Evans, D. (2012). *The art of walking.* London: Black Dog Publishing Limited; Ulrich, M., Hesse, F., & Oucherif, M. (Eds.). *Walk! Exhibition catalogue.* Vienna: Verlag für moderne Kunst

Fundamentally, walking becomes a way of doing research "to create a dynamic space/site for exploring, thinking, making, and speculating, where movement of the body and mind becomes deeply intertwined."[10] Recent publications aim at a decentering of "reductive notions of the able, humanist subject" and argue for education contexts "aligned with modes of collective attunement, micropolitical mobilization and 'side-by-side' movements into an uncertain future".[11] What all of these practices share is an interest in walking as embodied worldmaking and for how walking embeds us in diverse environments. This aligns with anthropologist Tim Ingold's strand of argumentation in his book on the production and significance of lines: Lines are generated through human practices – moving around, gesturing, speaking, and in creating in/visible traces in the (social) environment.[12]

But how are all of these practices embedded in the web of sociality?

Turning to the feminist researcher Sara Ahmed, we can inquire into this question with a queer-phenomenological approach to the social.[13] Rather than stating the sensory openness of bodies and their 'being toward the world' as a universal given, she re-reads traditional phenomenological thinking and carves out how perceptions and embodied experiences are powerfully oriented by their (socio-cultural) backgrounds. Transferred to the practice of walking, to 'arrive' somewhere can also be perceived as a manifestation of relations of proximity and distance in which normative or desired orientations become visible. Taking the 'background' of these orientations into account marks a shift in thinking about walking and the question of orientation: It brings to light the embeddedness of walking practices within sociocultural norms and necessitates a politics of space that take into account an intersectional approach and inquire into the social along axes of difference in their interdependence. Who walks – where? At what times of the day? At which pace? Is walking a leisure activity or a professional necessity in e.g. care services? How is walking also part of quantifying bodily practices and processes? What sensory de/sensibilizations are most prevalent in walking when we look at it from a gender-theoretical perspective? Following these questions, a phenomenological approach provides a fundamental reference point for a methodological approach to *walking as embodied world-making*.

Walking makes visible.

Walking has been widely researched and discussed including a large body of anthropological, philosophical, phenomenological, and methodological research. While walking can be addressed as a mode of inquiry, political intervention, or artistic practice, this book emphasizes that all of these practices share walking as an *embodied practice*. The contributions of this book are all located at the interface of analyzing walking as an aesthetic practice, within artistic research, and methodological questions offering inventive practices and sharp observations. With the focus on walking as embodied practice, the aesthetic dimension gains importance as a field of political, philosophical, and

---

10
Here in the connection with art/o/graphies: Lee, N. Y. S., Mosavarzadeh, M., Ursino, J. M., & Irwin, R. L. (2023). Introduction: Material and digital conversations: Walking matters in a/r/tography. In N. Y. S. Lee, M. Mosavarzadeh, J. M. Ursino, & R. L. Irwin (Eds.), *Material and digital a/r/tographic explorations: Walking matters* (Vol. 9, pp. 1–20). Studies in Arts-Based Educational Research. Singapore: Springer Nature

11
Lasczik et al., 2023, p.4

12
Ingold, T. (2007). *Lines: A brief history.* London: Routledge

13
Ahmed, S. (2010). *Queer phenomenology: Orientations, objects, others.* Durham: Duke University Press

educational inquiry into somatosensory experiences of actors that are always already involved, even entangled, with their environments – material and immaterial, human and more-than-human.[14]

Walking is always happening within, enveloped, and directed by specific environments and social contexts. All the diverse ways of walking share the relational quality between the body-in-movement and space constituted by the somatosensory impressions and continuous immersion of bodies into their environments. While we could frame this as responsiveness of bodies, it could also be captured as relations of touch "moving away from the seeming immediacy of an individualized cutaneous touch, moving simultaneously 'inwards' by complicating ideas of sensations throughout the dispersed body, but also 'outwards' between bodies and subjectivities".[15] The notion of touch reminds us of a body's situatedness within affective relations: to touch and be touched. The body is the nodal point of relations of touch through somatosensory impressions, material, and atmospheric environments. And in that way walking is a movement practice always connected to socio-material and affective environments. Walking can be a functional movement between places or a paced bridging of distances, a meandering, navigational tracing, traversing territories, etc. – and always comprises a suite of bodily performances. Through whichever means walking comes into view, it is always a situated and a continuous (re-)configuration of a shared space. Being in these spaces, and traversing them can be a methodological tool for generating knowledge about spaces and their inhabitants. And in that way, walking generates memories, pathways, encounters, relations, a bodily knowing… – it is worldmaking.[16]

The focus on embodiment leads to research approaches that trace walking in its culturally diverse forms of practice; it may also elicit a deeper interest in how bodies are conceptualized. Perhaps the most known accounts of that have been created by Marcel Mauss and Pierre Bourdieu who have developed the notion of the habitus that analyses bodies as situated within and shaped by societal conditions and their normative orders.[17] Bourdieu connects the societal and the individual through the concept of the habitus as an incorporated *practical sense* that emerges from being within social fields – it is embodied, displayed in the bodily hexis as a "durable way[s] of standing, speaking, walking, and thereby of feeling and thinking"[18] that are produced in the body's relations over time and in spatial arrangements. Perceived over time and in a very fundamental sense, the body is never only located in one or actual position but always the materialization of a trajectory – this is also of importance for accounting bodies as junction points of in/visible power structures that accumulate over time and materialize as embodied biographies.[19] With an interest in the act of walking, this sociological perspective elicits that

[14] Paterson, M., Dodge, M., & MacKian, S. (2016). Introduction: Placing touch within social theory and empirical study. In M. Paterson & M. Dodge (Eds.), *Touching space, placing touch*. London: Routledge, 1–28

[15] ibid., p. 7

[16] See also Careri, 2002; Pink, S., Hubbart, P., O'Neill, M., & Radley, A. (2010). Walking across disciplines: From ethnography to arts practice. *Visual Studies, 25*(1), 1–7; Pierce, J., & Lawhon, M. (2015). Walking as method: Toward methodological forthrightness and comparability in urban geographical research. *The Professional Geographer, 67*(4), 655–662; MacPherson, H. (2016). Walking methods in landscape research: Moving bodies, spaces of disclosure and rapport. *Landscape Research, 41*(4), 425–432; Edensor, T. (2010). Walking in rhythms: Place, regulation, style and the flow of experience. *Visual Studies, 25*(1), 69–79

[17] Mauss, M. (1973). Techniques of the body. *Economy and Society, 2*(1), 70–88

[18] Bourdieu, P. (1980). *The logic of practice*. Stanford: Stanford University Press, p. 69f

[19] Bodies are the expression of incorporated dispositions and therefore also markers of difference and exclusion, see Ennes, M. A. (2020). Bourdieu and the 'migrant-body': Embodiment in the migratory context. *Revista Brasileira de Sociologia, 8*(19), 26–58; Spahn, L. (2022). *Biography matters: Feministisch-phänomenologische Perspektiven auf Altern in Bewegung* [Biography matters: Feminist-phenomenological perspectives on ageing in motion]. Bielefeld: transcript

(social) pathways are the materialized memory of regular passages; they reveal habits and choices – or they conceal them. If we zoom into walking as a sequence of steps and footprints, visible or not, they are hinting at social orders "because knowing is doing, doing is carrying out tasks, and carrying out tasks is remembering the way they are done".[20]

[20] Ingold, T., & Vergunst, J. L. (Eds.). (2008). *Ways of walking: Ethnography and practice on foot.* Burlington: Ashgate, p. 7

We are not walking on surfaces but we are part of the spaces we walk in.

At the same time, walking artist Hamish Fulton reminds us as that those dominant spatio-temporal relations can be questioned, subverted, twisted. Walking as art can address and elucidate these dimensions. His artworks are "invisible objects" born from experiences; he states: "I transform ideas into physical experiences. My self-imposed rule is: If I do not walk I cannot make any art."[21] Walking as contemporary art interconnects the subjectively felt organism in the complex ecospheres we are part of. Cartography for example has been and is a powerful tool to mark territories according to specific signs and indicators. Maps not only propose walking paths, but they also orchestrate our experiences – they depict data from different locations into one comprehensive assemblage as navigational tool. However, deciding on a different way of moving through space can work as 'walking score' and become an artistic practice that creates or traces other lines than already established ones: Walking scores are open-ended propositions or invitations to walk in a specific way: listening to the sounds of the environment you walk in, looking for things of a specific color along the way, leaving a chalk trace,…

[21] Fulton, H. (2019). *Words from walks: Revised version VII.* URL: galerie-tschudi.ch/press/Words-from-Walks_Hamish-Fulton.pdf

And again, how do these ways of walking generate embodied experiences, make something visible, re-orient sensory habits or cross borders? How can those artistic practices re-orient our steps, create cartographies and provide navigational tools that resist the powerful culture of locating oneself through a bird's eye perspective? After all, we live in a digitalized age of (almost) permanent location. How, we might ask, can we then twist this data-based location through a politics of location (Adrienne Rich) that traces the situatedness of humans within social and geopolitical powerscapes?

In that way, walking – and generally moving – constitutes the world in somatosensory perceptions as it is an impregnated 'knowing through practice' through which we encounter environments. Walking takes diverse forms according to the specificity of the situation: a rhythmic walk when hiking, a slow balancing movement, a quick purposeful run to catch the train, or the monitoring movements of acts of observation. But ways of walking are also a connective force in space and time – they trace and connect memories, moments, and imaginations.[22]

[22] Ingold & Vergunst, 2008

And here lies the potential of methodologies and walking art[23]: They render visible, are means to expose (oneself to) established infrastructures or to analyse and twist 'acceptable' ways of walking. In walking-as-art, artists move themselves or material through spaces (sometimes otherwise

[23] For an historical overview in the field of the arts see: Careri, F. (2002). *Walkscapes: Walking as an aesthetic practice.* Barcelona: Editorial Gustavo Gili; Bassett, K. (2004). Walking as an aesthetic practice and a critical tool: Some psychogeographic experiments. *Journal of Geography in Higher Education, 28*(3), 397–410

inaccessible), often drawing attention to neglected, socially inherited, and habituated orders of perception. As a relational process and performative act, walking addresses the repercussions of our experiences that re-configure our moving bodies.

While this book takes the human body as a starting point it also wants to transgress anthropocentric accounts by highlighting the interdependence of the social and material space in complex ecological, material, socio-historical, technological, and geopolitical environments. Environments are constituted by the presence of others – humans, animals, plants, and other im/material traces in a more-than-human world. Thus, walking can also become a (critical) practice for becoming sensitive to the de/compositions of landscapes and (urban) environments at present.[24] This is mirrored in the thoughts of the anthropologists Tim Ingold and Jo Lee Vergunst who argue that walking is "to make one's way *through* a world-in-formation".[25] An example is Ingold's involvement with footprints: He stresses that they "have a temporal existence, a duration, which is bound to the very dynamics of the landscape to which they belong: to the cycles of organic growth and decay, of weather, and of the seasons".[26] And this takes us to another dimension of this book.

[24] Careri, 2002

[25] Ingold & Vergunst, 2008, p. 2, e.o.

[26] Ingold, T. (2010). Footprints through the weather-world: Walking, breathing, knowing. The Journal of the Royal Anthropological Institute, 16, 121–139

WALKING AS SPATIO-SENSUAL EXPERIENCE THAT IS (NEVER JUST) BOUND TO HERE

"Responding – being responsible/response-able – to the thick tangles of spacetimematterings that are threaded through us, the places and times from which we came but never arrived and never leave is perhaps what re-turning is about."[27]

The body of research brought about by feminist materialist thinking offers a striking shift for conceptions of the social.[28] As a diverse field, it elicits and negotiates new imaginaries for living in the Anthropocene.[29] Not only does it offer vivid analyses of the interdependent relationality of bodies of all kinds but this strand of thought assumes the agency of all matter and by that ignites a new perspective on the scope of social interaction. One of the central figures, quantum physicist and feminist theorist Karen Barad, questions conceptions of set boundaries and suggests a dynamic principle of intra-action, a re-configuration of different materialities and subjectivities in a continuous process of becoming.[30] In her approach, this intra-active performativity creates its own memory: "Memory – the pattern of sedimented enfoldings of iterative intra-activity – is written into the fabric of the world. The world 'holds' the memory of all traces; or rather, the world is its memory (enfolded materialisation)."[31] As this quote states, the world is considered as 'enfolded materialisation',

[27] Barad, K. (2010). Diffracting diffraction: Cutting together-apart. *Parallax*, 20(3), 168–187

[28] Alaimo, S., & Hekman, S. (Eds.). (2008). *Material feminisms*. Bloomington: Indiana University Press

[29] For a discussion of this contested term see: Haraway, D. J. (2015). Anthropocene, Capitalocene, Plantationocene, Chthulucene: Making kin. *Environmental Humanities*, 6, 159–165

[30] Barad, K. (2003). Posthumanist performativity: Toward an understanding of how matter comes to matter. *Signs: Journal of Women in Culture and Society*, 28(3), 802–831. URL: www.journals.uchicago.edu/doi/full/10.1086/345321

[31] Barad, 2010, p. 182

as an archive of traces that are continuously 'written' into the material world – of which human and non-human actors are part of. This also necessitates a reflection of conceptions of bodies as 'dispersed bodying' stressing the performativity of material entanglements across vast temporal and spatial scales.

We can enter this epistemological shift more deeply through the concept of 'trans-corporeality' by feminist materialist Stacey Alaimo.[32] It was developed from an environmental justice and health perspective that tracks and negotiates substances that move across and through bodies and places: "The subject as a material being, subject to the agencies of the compromised, entangled world, enacts an environmental posthumanism. The subject cannot be separated from networks of intra-active material agencies [...] and thus cannot ignore the disturbing epistemological quandaries of risk society".[33] Alaimo argues that taking the materiality of bodies into account renders tangible their entanglement with other material agencies. With a materialist perspective, she unfolds the idea that all beings are intermeshed with the material world they are made of, that crosses through and transforms them, and, in return, is transformed itself.[34] In this time of anthropogenic influences on planetary cycles and relations, the notion of transcorporeality connects biological, technological, political, and social dimensions. In this way, Alaimo also underscores the implicatedness of life on a planetary scale. Following materialist thinkers, we can question the dominant ways of looking at environments as 'natural other'. Going beyond anthropocentric conceptualizations of the social, a transcorporeal notion of the social calls for an 'ethico-politics' responsive to these conditions, as explicated by Astrida Neimanis in her posthuman phenomenology. She focuses on bodies "as both technological and ecological, connected up with other bodies of all kinds, and lived at diverse levels of sensory perception"[35] and thereby invites a broadening of perceptions and imaginations of bodies through a posthuman lens in which any kind of body is porous, dispersed, and imbricated in others.

We can inquire into walking from many perspectives. However, the reference to feminist and posthuman phenomenology sensitive to the situated and entangled existences that all beings share creates an analytical framework to reflect and engage in artistic practices and methodological entry points to walking. As a consequence, the book is a dialogue across disciplines, an example of post-disciplinary[36] research – in the sense of a laboratory for culturing new methodological approaches, methods, theories, and styles of writing. In bringing together a diverse range of research practices and theoretical accounts, the contributions transgress methodological terrains for an inquiry into the phenomenon of walking as an embodied and, movement-based field of research that connects ethnographic, aesthetic, phenomenological, and posthumanist entry points.

[32] Alaimo, S. (2008). Trans-corporeal feminism and the ethical space of nature. In S. Alaimo & S. Hekman (Eds.), *Material feminisms*. Bloomington: Indiana University Press, 214–236; Alaimo, S. (2018). Trans-corporeality. In R. Braidotti & M. Hlavajova (Eds.), *Posthuman glossary*. London: Bloomsbury, 435–438

[33] Alaimo, 2018, p. 436

[34] ibid.

[35] Neimanis, A. (2017). *Bodies of water: Posthuman feminist phenomenology*. London: Bloomsbury, pp. 26, 59

[36] Lykke, N. (2010). *Feminist studies: A guide to intersectional theory, methodology and writing*. New York: Routledge

ABOUT THE STRUCTURE OF THE BOOK

The contributions in this collection work with and through a variety of perspectives for perceiving and analysing walking and highlighting the interrelations of bodies, knowledges, places, affects, and other materialities.[37] This book illuminates the phenomenon of walking in four chapters – as a practice embedded in naturecultures[38] and contemporary powerscapes, as artistic practice, as a research methodology, and as a relational and performative practice situated in specific environments.

The decision for a transdisciplinary engagement with walking meant to invite a diversity of writing styles and forms of meaning-making. Navigating through the process of editing, I was inspired by questions like: How to convey embodied experiences? Which (kinds of) language or forms of expression can we engage in to share experiences and insights? How can this book become a space of inquiry through material, visual, and textual referentiality? And how does this book speak to the senses? Encouraging cross-disciplinary dialogue and a synergetic co-existence of different ways of capturing and evoking the sensuality, affectivity, materiality, and density of ways of walking, the contributions comprise a spectrum of writing styles and visual work that invites readers to access their own sensate, lived bodies while reading. Ranging from fiction to conceptual papers, to essays, and (visual) poetry the contributions will hopefully also inspire new perspectives and imaginations for future walks, pathways, and encounters.

The first part *Posthuman Imaginations – Walking in a More-than-Human World* is a (re-)consideration of walking along with posthuman and new materialist strands of thinking that have broadened our conceptions of bodies and environments considerably and created new sense-making fields.[39] As walking is a cultural practice that relies on an embodied experience and is always embedded in (social) environments, this chapter brings together contributions that engage with walking by inviting a sensibilization for the presence of others – for being among and part of the lively biosphere we inhabit together. Posthuman theories have highlighted not only the intricate entanglements of human and non-human life forms; in fact, they formulate a fundamental critique of anthropocentric and imperial ways of living that regard nature as 'other'. This distanced perspective becomes apparent in an extractivist logic that regards environments as resources, commodities, or territories. Critical posthumanism and vitalist materialisms in contrast conceive of a more-than-human world contesting traditional dichotomies of subject and object, culture and nature – and grand agency to non-human actors.[40] As mentioned before, the term naturecultures emphasizes that nature and culture cannot be separated and highlight the interrelatedness of human and non-human existences. Hence, also walking bodies need to be regarded as entangled in dynamically transforming relationships across and through bodies of all kinds. As Sarah Hennesey highlights: "Walking uncovers sparks for engagement

37 Instone 2013: 134

38 For an inspiring application of Donna Haraway's term of natureculture see: Gesing, F., Knecht, M., Flitner, M., & Amelang, K. (Eds.). (2017). *NaturenKulturen: Denkräume und Werkzeuge für neue politische Ökologien* [NatureCultures: Thinking spaces and tools for new political ecologies]. Bielefeld: transcript

39 Hamilton, J. M., & Neimanis, A. (2018). Composting feminisms and environmental humanities. *Environmental Humanities*, 10(2), 501–527

40 Coole, D., & Frost, S. (Eds.). (2010). *New materialisms: Ontology, agency, and politics*. Durham: Duke University Press; Hamilton, J. M., & Neimanis, A. (2018). Composting feminisms and environmental humanities. *Environmental Humanities*, 10(2), 501–527

within entangled worlds of the ecosystem."[41] For that reason, this chapter brings together very different ways of story-telling. The first contribution is a speculative rhythmic piece of storytelling in which the profession of *passers-by* is imagined. This contribution creates an *atmospheric cityscape* that is experienced through ephemeral moments of noticing and points at underlying normative orders. It may raise questions of what kinds of sensory sensorium the passers-by have developed or even how moving around is always – in some way – registered by co-present others. Inka°Witz contours the city as an almost fragile organism – raising questions of what makes cities a liveable space; where are neglected spaces; when do we avert our gaze from something, making it invisible; who and what shapes a city's face? This is contrasted with an interview with Mariele Weber who considers herself a *mediator between plants and humans*. Her perspective brings the (seemingly) stationary existence of plants into play with the cyclic rhythm of their seasonal transformation. Entering the perspective and temporality of plants may initiate an attentiveness to aliveness that is not necessarily at eye level but needs to be examined and experienced through changes in sensory experimentation and ways of moving – like crawling, lying, staying, looking up, climbing, etc. This is discussed further by Lea Spahn who introduces the notion of *bodyscapes* for a transcorporeal conception of bodies. Inspired by walking through the Czech-German national park Šumava as a group, the traversing of a landscape can elicit an embodied 'becoming-with' in *eco-affective environments*. This conceptual contribution is followed by *footnotes* by Astrid Lembcke-Thiel who offers a collage of her experiences, imaginations, memories, and associations taken with a smart phone while walking. Following her, we move across the pages that engender a visual texture and evoke the sensory immersion she experiences while walking – its durational experience of the body-in-movement and the ephemeral impressions that she perceives as *worldmaking*.

In the second chapter *Walking in the (Performative) Arts*, four artists present or re-contextualize their work within the framework of this book. Walking art has become a field for aesthetic and political engagement with the conditions and concepts that shape our (built) environments and the worldmaking possibilities of artistic practices.[42] Walking art is related to contemporary societal discourses and lifeworlds; and even more, walking artists engage their own (or other) bodies, make visible and challenge normalized conceptions of walking: They contrast and amplify as they make visible what otherwise may be unnoticed. One figure of reference is Charles Baudelaire's *flâneur* who was conceived as a leisurely strolling observer of modern urban life (today also criticized as a bourgeois, white, male figure). Another known example of walking arts is the collective and avant-garde group Situationist Internationale who recast walking through the concept of *dérives*. They used walking as 'psychogeographical' re-encounters with post-war urban surroundings in the 20th century.[43] The thereby created experimental scores were also an engagement in which dominant knowledge and capitalist logics of city planning were disrupted and re-placed in experience-based and subjective mappings by allowing them to be 'drawn into the terrain'. Contemporary walking artists address discourses of living

41 Hennesey, S. (2023). Anecdotal edges: Propositions from sketching the walk as a post-humanist research method. In Lasczik et al., 2023, p. 87

42 Interestingly, the Schirn Kunsthalle in Frankfurt am Main (Germany) has curated the exhibition *Walk!* which presents walking artists from all around the globe: https://www.schirn.de/ausstellungen/2022/walk/

43 Careri, 2002

– and walking – in late-capitalist global societies criticizing e.g. the unequally distributed privilege of free-roaming or migration, the normative orders/restricted access for bodies that are 'othered' or 'dis-abled', they cast light on perceptive processes while walking as a specific pace to move through landscapes or the interaction with biological and material environments, or engage with the increasing surveillance of public space.[44] In the past years, another influential force has been the pandemic situation with its vast effect on artistic practice and (im)possible formats of performing; this has sparked the development of virtual, present, or delegated walks (and works) that became a medium to continue, translocate and share the work.[45] This diversity of artistic works on walking is mirrored by the four artists present in this book who take up the question "why walking?" with their own walking bodies. In the first contribution, Antonín Brinda presents his work *(Dis-)Obedient Walking, (Dis)Obedient Riding*. In his walks, he enters the built logic of megacities by moving through their transportation network. Moskow, Ulanbataar, and Bejing are the three sites of performative walks, bus or train rides to 'articulate' the cities' transportation systems as precisely as possible. Following that, ANa Anaa reflects on herartistic research centered around walking in the industrial area of Brest (France) and its inflictions on bodies. The exposure of the body to this built environment leads to an unescapable experience of exhaustion and liminality that becomes her starting point for developing the notion of *Bodies of Transit* referring to the circulation of (toxic) substances through bodies both human and nonhuman. This interaction with a specific environment is also present in Hana Magdoňová's performative work staying *39 days* in the former quarry Hády in Brno (Czechia). She vividly captures the different ways of walking in the lowest plain – exploring the ground, measuring, dancing, sensing, or collecting trash – and reports the attunement of her body to the minute transformations of the biodiverse environment. The slow renaturation process of a human-made landscape becomes tangible through close attention to daily cycles and weather changes by staying present. In the final contribution of this chapter, Otto Kauppinen takes us to *immersive theater* productions. He gives a close description of two pieces during the festival CAMPQ in Prague in 2019 where the audiences became part of the theatrical worldbuilding. His analysis reveals the potential of contemporary artistic practices to create *temporary communities through shared activities* like walking or eating. From that perspective, artistic practices are potential sites of the *'emergence of relations'* as he argues with Nicolas Bourriaud and the political impact of shared time in individualized and privatized societies.

The third chapter offers a *methodological perspective on walking* as a way of doing research that facilitates a connection to lived experiences that are embodied and sedimented biographical journeys and memories but also related to spaces, communities, and politics of identity. Walking not only relies on the vital body as means of research but it can also address exactly this capacity to be corporeally involved, affected, and attuned to the situatedness and perspectivity of lived experiences.[46] An example is Andreea Racles' research on belonging

[44] For an overview, see: Oucherif, M. (2022). Why walk? In M. Ulrich, F. Hesse, & M. Oucherif (Eds.), *Walk! Exhibition catalogue*. Vienna: Verlag für moderne Kunst, 175–179

[45] This was reflected by: Osicková, K., Brinda, A., & Dlouhý, P. (Eds.). (2021). *Remote performance art: Performance Crossings 2020 and the disappearance of live performance*. Praha: powerprint

[46] For further explication of this lifeworld ethnography that discusses perspective and the bodily involvement of researchers see: Kotthaus, V., & Weste, N. (2021). In P. Eisewicht, R. Hitzler, & L. Schäfer (Eds.), *Der soziale Sinn der Sinne: Die Rekonstruktion sensorischer Aspekte von Wissensbeständen* [*The social meaning of the senses: Reconstructing sensory aspects of knowledge*]. Wiesbaden: VS

and transnational lives of a Rom*ja woman in Spain in which she traces the empowering potential of walking as an ethnographic method that combines that materiality and corporeality of movement with a sensibilization for the routes and places of people in their concreteness.[47] As a method(ology), walking can become a 'walking with', "requiring from the ethnographer to adjust her/his pedestrian movements to the movements of who is guiding" and questioning "who holds the knowledge and the position of making it available to the ethnographer", as she points out.[48] This is also highlighted by O'Neill and Hubbart who perceive walking as a methodology that relies on the "sharing of sensuous, kinaesthetic experiences" by which the attunement to another's perspective becomes an embodied experience and in that way also potentially a collaborative site of knowledge-production.[49] In this way, walking is a performative method for understanding lived experience within axes of social inequality that encompass felt and lived experiences, memories, and imaginations.[50] We could relate this also to Judith Butler's work on the assembly as a performative appearance or formation of bodies in public space: She argues that these assemblies not only render visible the vulnerability of bodies and the precarity of lives but can become a performative form of political resistance by creating new relations in the now.[51] Relating to these ideas, the contributions of this chapter exemplify walking as a method(ology) in different fields. In the first contribution, Shira Wachsmann presents her work on *War Trauma, Embodiment, and the Re-Membering of Matter*. She applies Karen Barad's agential realism to the experience of explosions and the vast effects this has on re-membering as a continuous re-enactment of matter and meaning in a conflictive war zone. Following this, Marie Kammler presents the *Science of Strollology* developed by Lucius and Helga Burghardt as a political and embodied method for city planning in motorized cityscapes. In specific artistic interventions and community-based work, the 'right of way' for pedestrian movement can be negotiated and effect a change in future planning. The third contribution is an inventive application of walking as an approach for *feminist research in urban spaces* from three perspectives: Maja Maksimović, Darija Medić, and Mirjana Utvić each propose *sensory encounters* that are captured in visually and narrative accounts that aim at giving insights into their embodied experience of spatial infrastructures.

The last chapter focuses on *situated experiences while walking* – attuning and attending to the embodied experience of specific environments and practices of walking. Here, we return to the framing given in the first part of the introduction: Walking as embedded social practice in lifeworlds and practice of worldmaking in the sense of constituting (shared) experiences. Especially the situatedness and perspectivity of body-bound activities become apparent in these contributions; in walking, specific subjectivities and their practice-based knowledge emerge.[52] Dorothea Hamilton gives a vivid impression of *highlining when walking on a 2.54 cm wide line*. She not only describes her dealing with the existential fear of falling as a beginner in highlining but also the gendered culture in the community. While this contribution deals with the embodied

[47] Racles, A. (2020). Walking with Lina in Zamora: Reflections on Roma's home-making engagements from a translocality perspective. *Intersections: East European Journal of Society and Politics*, 4(2), 86–108

[48] Ibid., p. 95

[49] O'Neill & Hubbart, 2010, p.50

[50] Ibid., p. 48

[51] Butler, J. (2015). *Notes toward a performative theory of assembly*. Cambridge: Harvard University Press

[52] Practice Theory has become a widely applied research methodology that focuses on situational actor constellations in their co-constitutive performativity; analyses foreground social practices as material-semiotic interfaces rather than restricting the social to human interactions. See Schatzki et al. 2001

experience of gravity and the heightened awareness of each step while balancing, the following text is a contrasting account of *long-distance hiking* in the Pyrenees. Susanne Nemmertz captures bivouacking as a relational spacemaking of bodies-in-movement and the perceptive attunement to the environment in accord with the need e.g. for places to stay overnight. Another spatial experience is presented by the artistic duo Zündwerk: During the pandemic, when social togetherness was highly regulated, Regula Pöhl and Daniela Villinger decided to *walk toward each other. Every Wednesday* depicts this interest in the towardness with a strong visual approach to this worldmaking between two moving bodies. The final contribution by Eva Clara Tenzler is a poetic text rich in sensory impressions and situational associations that capture the experience of walking uphill. *Gehen* is the delicate interweaving of words and their metaphorical horizon. Some parts of the text are translated by physical poet Shannon Sullivan inviting the reader to use them as walking scores: The short captivations can be read as tasks for walking practices based on subjective interpretation. The book closes with this invitation to go out and walk – connecting to the breathing body-in-movement, noticing the changes in weather, grounds, and environments, and perhaps with a new curiosity for walking as socio-political practice.

ACKNOWLEDGMENTS

Working on this book has felt like curating as it brings together contributions from different fields and artistic/research practices that all have their unique ways of sharing experiences, insights, and reflections. I am indebted to a diverse body of writing on walking that has shaped and inspired this book through strikingly inventive and observant reflections hoping that this book will also be a sensory experience and elicit new perspectives on the phenomenon of walking.

I want to thank all contributors for their insightful work and the collaborative communication over the whole process. I want to give a special thank you to Kristýna Krejčová and Kristýna Žáčková who have created the graphic design for this book. Starting from the question of what kind of experience this book should be for the readers, the cooperation was a truly delightful quest!

The book would not have manifested without the generous financial support of the publication grant I received from the Faculty of Fine Arts at the Brno University of Technology – I am very grateful for this opportunity! I want to express my thanks to Ladislav Jackson for bridging language barriers in the application process. And I want to thank Lenka Vesela for her encouraging and collegial support in preparing the first edition of this book.

This book is an outcome of my research residency at the Faculty of Fine Arts in 2021 when I arrived to Brno into a lockdown due to the Corona pandemic. During this time of virtual communication and learning environments, I was welcomed to be present in the institution's space to dive into my research – very much accompanied by walks discovering this new place and developing the idea for this book further while being in movement.

For this first edition, this introduction has been revised and ideas for a sequence have grown. These days, I have been wandering through my neighborhood and surrounding fields discovering a new side of walking. On my body, I carry a child, a warm body breathing along with me. My hands are resting on the little body, protective but also reassuring myself that, yes, he is there. And the perception of my surroundings has changed: I watch the world with a new attentiveness. My steps…slower, a new rhythm. I follow my feet, decide where to go simply while walking – the distance is measured in breastfeeding rhythms. Winter turned into spring while walking, and I have experienced the incremental changes of a season – from gazing into wintery branches reaching into the skies above muddy paths to the first sprouts and wild flowers, and finally the blossoming of cherry trees and a whole spectrum of greens. I hope, you as readers will enjoy the contributions and let them take you on very different walks.

Brno & Marburg, April 2025

Posthuman Imaginations – Walking in a More-than-human World

inka°witz
Passers-by*

* Passers-by are pioneering individuals creating liveliness. You will recognize them, you will notice life when you see it. Intend to do that!¹

1
Editor's note: Pioneering translates to the German word "wegweisend" which also means "leading the way".

When the fog lifted, there was a landscape and in the landscape, a city.
There was tumult and wasteland and tire wear and lost things. A glove
beside a trough, an eraser on the asphalt, a water bottle in a crack.

> The city is the ground on which passing becomes possible. The passers-by
> depend on this ground, and this ground only becomes a city through the
> passers-by. Passing is like tracing a labyrinth with a pencil, only denser
> and with more gaps in between.

Every now and then a conversation mumbles by like

I was so excited my heart jumped out of my pocket.

> This city is beautiful. But that's not all. This city is well thought out. There
> is some caring about space, the space and time we share. Many do not
> even know that there are passers-by. They are quiet, almost secret. They
> are everywhere. Their job is to balance the atmosphere. Here, now, this
> place for example. This hurried crowd also needs a slowness. A passer-by
> recognizes this immediately. She will take care of this gap and be slow.
> You will notice it, not consciously, it will be a triviality to you. She will
> move slowly and prudently and it will remind you of something.

A pink pom-pom of a once-beloved cap on paved.

> *Who needs such a thing?*

Islands of language, surfaces of silence, spaces of noise.

> Walking is a self-prolonging into the world. It is something that some have
> learned. The bodies act so differently; some send their heads ahead, others
> seem to grind seeds with their hips, still, others dream of icy surfaces
> with their feet. The walking continues in the head. An embodied process.

The city is open at the ends, like a braided pigtail without a hair tie.
This is important.

> Here's a tip: When you get out of
> a truck at night,
> you have to be careful that you judge
> the height correctly, otherwise
> it can hurt your knees.

There are many reasons why there are passers-by. Passers-by are people who make passing possible. A passing from person to person. On the street, on the corner, at the railroad crossing, in the park, on bridges and squares, in the periphery of the city, in the core of the city. They get a decent salary. It is enough to live on.

> Perhaps they differ from the others because the walking of the others is directed, has personal goals. Their walking is justified in the process itself.

Cartography of reality.

> The traces. Here, someone has walked through paint and another and another. An imprint held in the tar for a quarter of an eternity. Yesterday's feet. We too have been here, walked here.

Here's a tip: Never walk behind
a person who is afraid
on the sidewalk. Change the side of the street.
In peace, there is room for it.

> The moment at the traffic light, where everything stands shortly in red, stands still in red, the red before the next green. This moment drips with potential. A common intention.

And go!

> Some cities cannot cope with the demands for diversity with their resident population and call in reinforcements. The city force does its duty and enhances the cityscape. Here in this city, they exist. A trained eye will recognize them. They recognize each other, share this mission; passing in/occurring to the city.

What happens is very different.

The city is full of oddities, full of lived lives. They are just some of them.

> The one who always walks from east to west in the morning seems to test the earth's gravity with her steps, inch by inch. Walks the city like research. The feet testify to the elemental force of physics and that reassures them. Inch by inch. The next day anew from east to west. Like that other one. You know.

Here's a tip: If you want to think, then walk,
divide the landscape in two,
connected by your directedness You will become
another when you have gone.

> One of them once set out and went out in the morning to work, walked through the city, reached the center and there was a lack of 'longing for somewhere', so she started walking. She passed the center, got into the ring, walked through the popular neighborhoods, to the periphery and beyond, then into the fields, the meadows, walked under the highway bridge, that's how it's told, and on and on. She walked and walked and still walks, because there, in the city center, the 'longing for somewhere' was missing. She does her job with a true sense of duty. Those of the city continue to pay her, even if she is no longer seen here. But she is missing and a gap is also a part of something. Now she is somewhere, passing a barrier or a national border and is still a passer-by, you don't stop being that.

The first sentence you say now is a lie, the second is true and from then on only lies.

> It's true, the city is always a potential ruin, it knows that it can happen, that the blooming can stop abruptly or insidiously. Always. But not now, not yet, not for a long while yet, everything in moderation. We have time.

The walking,
the rushing,
the running,
the strolling and promenading,
the following,
the leading,
the guiding,
the tapping,
The wandering and sauntering,
the hastening,
the dwelling,
they all are disciplines.

> One who walks bent over, almost at a right angle from the third thoracic vertebrae to the ground, will rarely see the sky. He walks like a meter. He is not one of the paid ones.

> An old woman walking in her husband's suit. He is no longer there, only his suit. The shoulders too broad, the pants too long, the belt barely fits around the round of her middle. She gives this scene a grace, a dignity, a respect. In truth, there are no universal signs of love.

When two meet in their everyday cityscape-keeping stroll, they barely greet. See each other and only know and know that there is no need for signs. A silent agreement.

One keeps looking into the windows. Everything becomes merchandise in her gaze.

Others twitch like lightning through the streets, hardly there, already gone.

I imagined it quite differently, somehow bigger.

Here's a tip: If you have nothing to give,
don't look at them. Keep your gaze
at your eye level. That saves
hope. In looks, there is always an ounce
of hope. That cannot be changed.

Life led on a leash gropes along winding paths.

Lost things are many. Bodies also are lost on the roads and paths. Lying on the edge as if they had slipped out of a piece of luggage, slid to the ground, and had to be found.

Someone sprayed an 0800 number on the wall there on the shotcrete. If called, there would be a mail-order company at the end with friendly advice.

So much for that.

Passers-by are brought into the city. They swarm out and swarm in again. They can't live there, they would lose their objectivity.

Everything becomes broadband. Runs sideways past left and right. The front view splits, splits into two film strips.

Here and there the herd is spat out at times. It splits only gradually. The paths cut the group into slices, into individual parts. The tempos detach the fragments of people from each other and let them stand or walk for themselves.

Somewhere it must be, I have put it here in these

It is also the case that there was a passer-by who misinterpreted her assignment and leaned towards change. It was an impulse that had been dormant in her for a long time. A throbbing longing that slowly pushed the limit of what was desirable. Actually, they are not supposed to do anything but passing. The one we are talking about here started with small beauty interventions. A candy wrapper was picked up by her, as if accidentally, and placed where it could shine. This small act made her so happy that she wanted to change bigger things. The light of a street lamp was colored in red. Matter of taste you will say now, and yes, it is, and they are not allowed to do that. They are not allowed to change the space, the urban space by rearranging it. They are allowed to pass here. But it went further than that. She moved crosswalks, she rerouted a small branch of the river, and eventually, she even moved houses, replaced roofs, and screwed with the slope of the hills and mountains. The damage was immense. You can guess. The city was outraged. She was fired and taken back in a truck to where she belonged.

> The non-walking. The standing is a resistance. The non-walking is a protest. Staying is a cruel privilege of the stronger.

Children are also among them. Their steps warn to avoid the cracks. Even the small ones. They jump from surface to surface in order not to slide into the ground, under the earth. There you can only lie, not jump.

> If passing here was no longer possible, then everyone would get in these trucks and go to the open ends of the city and out and into the countryside. If passing here was no longer possible, maybe the ends would be cut off beforehand, so tightly that not even the fields could become pathways.

If there were no more passers-by, maybe something would fall from the sky, the daughter of a goddess, or a meteorite, or an explosive device like a bomb, or big news, and anyway, there would be a big smoke, and then the beginning of another story would have to be here.

> Sometimes this happens

When the smoke cleared, there was no longer a city, only a landscape, a wasteland, a skeleton. A center in the process of dissolution. Lost was time and all things, a trough where before there was no trough. A crack where once a road, a crack.

Mariele Weber
"Another Gaze" – Seeing the World from the Perspective of a Plant

Interviewed by Lea Maria Spahn

Lea: This book is about different ways of moving through the world as a human being in general and with all the consequences: that through our movement, the world is also in motion, that we come into contact with things, leave things behind, always influenced, perhaps even navigated, through social practices and their orders but also through direct encounters. In this way, we can understand the social as a sensual and relational encounter, as an entanglement. The phenomenological perspective provides an approach to this embodied experience of being on the move with very different senses – be it listening to the echo of our own footsteps in our bodies or entering into an encounter with the world visually, through smells or, as in your case, also with the sense of taste. We often see 'at eye level' or from a human-centered gaze, as we move through the world. But when we set out with a shifted attention, this might take us to different experiences and encounters. With that in mind, my first question to you is: You work as an herbal pedagogue; how would you describe that profession yourself – and what does it mean to you?

Mariele: First and foremost, I see myself as a pedagogue. I identify very strongly with this role. However, the term herb does not go far enough for me. I work a lot with the term wild plant pedagogue. But I also work with cultivated plants in my garden pedagogical work. Therefore, I could also open up the terms completely and call myself a plant pedagogue. Perhaps I rather perceive myself as a mediator between plants and people, as many herbalists perceive themselves.

L: So if you understand yourself as mediator between people and plants, what does that mean exactly and how did you come to this profession?

M: I have studied this field in a certain way and gained experience in it. Because I have learned to understand the world of plants a little better than other people who have not studied it as intensively, I grew to become a mediator. In the beginning, I was mainly concerned with garden and cultivated plants, also with the aim of growing vegetables or herbs. Then I discovered the wild plants, especially the edible ones, because as my knowledge of the classic garden vegetables grew, my view opened up and I asked myself what I could actually eat while hiking. In this way, new areas of the plant world came into my life: medicinal plants, dying plants; I also began to interact and look at plants on completely different levels with questions like: 'How do plants influence me?'. So I now look at plants from very different angles and hardly ever do I not see something exciting and instructive in a plant. Thus, I think I know them quite well or know how to approach plants. I see it as my task, also with regard to climate and nature protection and the inglorious role that humans play here, namely, a destructive one, to work against this and to do educational work. To be a mediator means to be a person who brings people into contact with plants. A quote from "The Little Prince" by Antoine de Saint-Exupéry comes to my mind: "All your life you are responsible for what you have made yourself familiar with." That's how I feel about plants.

L: Can you reach out once again and describe a little closer what your path has been up until now?

M: During my voluntary ecological year, I had my first encounters with wilderness and outdoor education. These were my first encounters with a pedagogy in which people consciously work with people and nature. Through my work with a non-governmental organization with a focus on political education and global learning, I became strongly involved in nature and climate protection and got to know many initiatives in this field. After that year, I studied environmental education in Vienna. In this course of studies, I learned to see myself as a mediator between nature and people. My training was, so to speak, actively engaging for and with the environment and advising people on how to find more environmental- and climate-friendly ways to interact. In my work in various educational initiatives, during and after my studies, I often realized that I was not reaching people with the issues of climate and nature conservation, which often seemed difficult and oppressive for everyone involved, whether participants or speakers. I wondered how I could reach people, how I could design the topics so that they could take root and encourage people at the same time. That's how I ended up in social work, especially adventure and outdoor education, because this field is primarily concerned with people, group dynamics and the individual. So in order to be able to mediate between nature and people, I also had to learn to understand people better. Adventure and outdoor education, which I studied in Marburg, helped me with this. In recent years, I have added further training in the field of wild plant pedagogy which has allowed me to focus on plants in my work as an educator. That's how it all came about: first the environment, then the people, then the plants. Now, I believe I understand these three well and can relate them to each other.

L: You see yourself as a mediator and do a lot of educational work. That means you have different fields of activity; on the one hand, you are an independent herbal pedagogue, on the other hand you also work in a gardening association. What are the differences in your working methods?

M: In the gardening association, we see ourselves as an educational garden and offer various community garden groups and events around agricultural policy issues and organic gardening. I am responsible for the children's project and regularly offer gardening for various school classes. This is very much learning by doing, so this pedagogical work is hands-on. In addition to my work in the educational garden, it was important for me to pursue my own independent path as a wild plant pedagogue. Here, my focus is very much on reaching multipliers in addition to my work with children and young people. In my role as a wild plant educator I am always searching for ways to generate points of contact with one's co-world.

L: You just changed from the term "Umwelt" to "Mitwelt" in German, which is a change from an anthropocentric understanding of environment or as separate from humans to an understanding of a co-world in which humans understand themselves as incremental parts of environment. Why is that shift meaningful to you?

M: By changing a term, we influence our attitude. There is an interaction between the term and the attitude. For me, it triggers a completely different attitude when I say co-world to my surroundings instead of environment. The environment is something that surrounds the human being as a subject, whereas with the term "co-world" (Mitwelt), we understand ourselves as part of it. To me, co-world conveys a greater belonging of myself to plants and animals and everything in between. The term environment distances me as a human being or sets me apart from it. The shift in a term also shifts the relationship, as Geseke von Lüpke describes it.[1] A big step in raising awareness towards an ecological ethic is this shift from environment to co-world.

[1] Von Lüpke, G. (2015). Conference: Into the Nature, Friedrichswalde, Germany, 7–18 April 2015, p. 7.

L: In English, there is not only the term "being toward to world" (Merleau-Ponty), but "being of the world" (Haraway), that is, being part of it. That's what I find exciting, that terms not only change an attitude, but also perception in general and how I locate myself within the world. And I'm entering into the topic of walking now. If we were to go on a walk together as part of your educational work, what would happen? Where would we go and how exactly would we move, what would we do?

M: One thing is very important to me in my educational offerings when I work as a wild plant pedagogue is 'being on our way'. In the educational garden, we are always in a fixed place and I bring people in touch with the garden, make this place accessible to them. But a lot of my work as a wild plant pedagogue is about wild plants and not about the plants that were planted in the garden so we can work with them. The garden has its advantages but for me, wild plants are about opening my eyes to my co-world. That's why it is very important for me to go to the people I work with so that they get to know their immediate surroundings and the spaces in which they move on a day-to-day basis. That is one thing. The other is, of course, being on the way together and opening our senses with small methodical approaches. That's why I perceive myself also as a pedagogue, because methodologies provide me with important support and should also provide the participants with support. It can be a small beginning, in which you go into your surroundings with a search assignment: "Find a plant that appeals to you in some way. You don't have to know the plant, you don't have to know the name. Look around, take your time, and then come back with that plant, or better yet, take us to that plant. Maybe give it an imaginary name." In this way, I get the participants to look at the plant more closely and let it cause something, associations for example. It should take off the pressure to already arrive with knowledge about the course in the classical scientific way, being already knowledgeable about the plant before you have even looked at it.

For me, it's about getting to know the plants in a very open and playful way, looking at your surroundings in a very open-minded way, using all your senses. In this way, we would start by getting to know our co-world and the world of plants together.

> L: I'm interested in this way of moving around or the way we engage sensually with the world as embodied beings. You said that we go to the plant or bring the other participants to the plant. It sounds like your work is about giving up one's own point of view, perhaps moving somewhere else. Figuratively speaking, you initiate a process by asking the participants to give up their points of view, to take on a new perspective. How else do you initiate the encounter? If I enter this situation, I imagine I may have to bend down, I may have to touch the plant, smell it, taste it.

M: Exactly. Quite often, I also give tasks that are precisely about broadening one's perspective. What I observe, if one does not deal much with plants and their purpose, is that people quite often only look at striking leaves or blossoms and do not pay attention to the rest of the plant. We often only perceive a fraction of the whole. Quite often I get a photo where only a leaf or a flower is to be seen and I am asked: "What kind of plant is this?" It doesn't occur to people that there are plants which have similar blossoms or leaves. If you compare this to the perception of animals, it seems absurd: You don't remember only the head of a fox. You also know what the tail looks like or the approximate body structure. But in addition to that, plants change over the course of the year. And that is not portrayed; we simply have a lack of pictures of that. I find that very fascinating. I also like to give the task to look at all visible features of the plant, and then to go further, not only perceiving them with the eyes, but also to feeling, smelling, tasting and finding – perhaps even inventing – terms for them. Did you know that the human eye can perceive 100 000 shades of color? We often only name color ranges: Green, blue, yellow, etc. And depending on the regions we grew up in, we have differentiated terms for each color. In our latitudes, we have many terms for shades of green: moss green, grass green, lime green or fir green, to name a few. In other regions, desert regions for example, people have many terms for different shades of brown or yellow. I can recommend practicing naming the perceived color nuances, to train perception. By finding terms for what we see, feel or smell, our perception also expands. So this interacts with each other. With this example we see that it is helpful to find terms for color tones in order to be able to perceive color nuances more consciously. And this is how I generally try to work with plants as well, to encourage participants to find terms for what, for example, the leaf of a pungent plant feels like or tastes like. For this, to come back to the beginning of your question, you have to change perspectives, your point of view and turn towards the plant.[2]

2 Arendt, H. (2017). *Werkstatt Pflanzenfarben – Natürliche Malfarben selbst herstellen und anwenden* [*Studio plant-based colours – Making and using natural paints yourself*]. Baden & München: AT Verlag, p. 40

> L: I remember you once named "weeds" in urban space in Marburg, Germany, during a joint action with a friend. What would you say is special about dealing with wild plants or often named "weeds"?

M: Again, we can make a difference by altering a name, so whether I say "wild plant" or "weed". This action was part of an international movement, known as #morethanweeds[3]. A grassroots movement of botanists that first emerged in the UK and France and became known in Germany as #Krautschau[4] or #MehrAlsUnkraut.[5] In 2020, you could find loads of pictures in the internet that reported such actions. So I set out in the old town of Marburg with my friend to name some wild plants, the so-called weeds, between curbs and walls with chalk. We wanted to raise awareness for these plants since especially in the sealed urban space, wild plants are strongly displaced. But despite all this, they always find their ways to grow, which I find very impressive. That was important to us, to make visible, to name these plants, to raise awareness that they are not simply weeds but, for example, that a dandelion is just fighting its way through the asphalt.

[3] More than Weeds. *About More than Weeds: The project*. URL: https://morethanweeds.co.uk/the-project

[4] Schwägerl, C. (2020). *Krautschau: Pflanzenfans machen die Vielfalt der Arten mit Kreide sichtbar* [*Krautschau: Plant fans make species diversity visible with chalk*]. In: *RiffReporter*. URL: https://www.riffreporter.de/de/umwelt/krautschau-botanik-vielfalt-pflanzen

[5] More than Weeds. *About More than Weeds: In other countries*. URL: https://morethanweeds.co.uk/in-other-countries/

Gelber Lerchensporn, yellow larksporn in Marburg, Germany

L: In particular, this naming and visualizing, perhaps also opening and changing the perception of how people move through their space: seems to be a concern of yours. What inspires you?

M: In the last few years, a relatively large amount of literature has been published, for example, about the rights of plants, trying to understand our world through the perspective of plants – plant philosophy like Emanuele Coccia with his book "The Roots of the World".[6] Plants are as fundamental a part of this earth as animals and humans but are often not given the same importance. Stefano Mancuso, an Italian plant scientist, deals a lot with these issues in his work and in his latest book "The Rights of Plants".[7]

L: So these are very different perspectives on plants as living beings that are being proposed.

M: Yes, for example, the discussions about neophytes[8], a so-called invasive species or 'immigrant plants'. Some people, even people who work intensively with plants, are of the opinion that neophytes, such as the Canadian goldenrod or the Indian knapweed, are undesirable plants. Some argue they do not belong to the native plants or to the original native plants and take away their habitat. I have a completely different attitude. On the one hand, because I see it in comparison to humans. Who has the right to immigrate here? For me, everyone has the right to go where they desire to, to have the opportunity to live a good life. For me it is no different with plants. Moreover, I feel it is an arrogant anthropocentric attitude and limited view of the plants' life form. Since their existence, they colonize the world and travel it in most creative ways. Stefano Mancuso has also published a very descriptive book on this subject: "The Incredible Journey of Plants".[9] A classic example of how humans participate in the spread of plants is the journey of the potato. Originally from the South American mountainous Andean regions, the potato found its way to Europe in the 16th century with European sailors and is now one of our favorite staple foods.[10] In view of the fact that the climate is changing, plants must also learn to adapt to it. However, at the rate of man-made climate change, this presents a huge, almost impossible challenge for many of our native plants. Thus, in the future, more plants will establish themselves that were not previously native to our latitudes. There is also more talk of a shift in vegetation zones as a result of climate change. So the question really is: What is native and what is not? Where does one start in the journey? Plants have always been on the move, finding the most creative ways to get around. They made the world liveable for humans and animals in the first place, laying the groundwork for us to breathe at all – co-founding our atmosphere.[11]

---

6 Coccia, E. (2021). *Die Wurzeln der Welt: Eine Philosophie der Pflanzen* [*The roots of the world: A philosophy of plants*]. München: dtv.

7 Mancuso, S. (2021). *Die Rechte der Pflanzen* [*The rights of plants*]. Stuttgart: Verlag Klett-Cotta.

8 Wittig, R., & Streit, B. (2004). *Ökologie* [*Ecology*]. Stuttgart: UTB basics, Verlag Eugen Ulmer, p. 211.

9 Mancuso, S. (2020). *Die unglaubliche Reise der Pflanzen* [*The incredible journey of plants*]. Stuttgart: Verlag Klett-Cotta, p. 115.

10 Seidel, W. (2012). *Die Weltgeschichte der Pflanzen* [*The world history of plants*]. Köln: Eichborn Verlag, p. 185.

11 Coccia, E. (2018). *Die Wurzeln des Lebens: Eine Philosophie der Pflanzen* [*The roots of life: A philosophy of plants*]. München: Hanser, p. 15.

L: Yes, this reminds me very much of Emanuele Coccia, who talks about a total immersion in the process of breathing and about the shared breath of the most diverse living beings, which are interdependently connected to each other.

M: That opens an exciting topic, a particular direction in approaching plants. I indicated at the beginning that I approached plants step by step; with each new perspective, I got to know plants anew from different directions. I like to describe this as pair of glasses. First, I wore the glasses for cultivated plants and scanned my world for exactly these plants and places. Then I gained another pair of glasses and got to know more and more plants, namely edible wild plants. After that, I entered the world of medicinal plants, then the dye plants, and so on. So more and more plant worlds have opened up to me. And now, I no longer see it as a pair of glasses that I put on, but as a filter that I have taken off. I walk through the world and see plants everywhere and can only filter with difficulty. My world looks very green. In my courses, I have often been asked what it is like for me to harvest a plant. I always state clearly that it depends on the attitude with which I harvest the plant. If I go into an encounter with the plant, I will not harvest it completely. However, if I approach it with the attitude of wanting to use it, it happens much more quickly that I harvest large quantities, so that the plant is no longer well. Another very new view on the plant world, in which I have discarded further filters, is that I perceive plants as a counterpart, as a dialogue partner in the sense of nature coaching through which I can learn something about myself. This is comparable to animal-assisted therapy which should be a familiar concept to many.

L: What can we learn from plants if we take off our filters or even encounter them as dialogue partners?

M: When people notice or have respect for a plant, try to respond to it, ask what it is related to, I encourage them to look for associations and metaphors to find out what the underlying themes may be. Here is a very personal example: I noticed thistles a lot last year. Even in the spring, I found the leaf rosettes to be incredibly beautiful and was surprised myself because I hadn't noticed thistles in this way before. Throughout the year I observed them and perceived even the faded and brown thistles in autumn and winter as beautiful and aesthetic. So I began to engage with this resonance. I asked myself what associations I have, what properties I assign to them, researched what their healing power is, and collected what I found about thistles in various literature. Following Paracelsus' theory of signatures, I found many topics that suited at that time: The growth and thorns of thistles are associated with protection and defensiveness.[12] This resonated with me at that time. And this example may illustrate how I interact with people in their plant encounters. When I go out with people, I encourage them to pay attention when plants keep catching their eye and what this might mean for them. In popular medicine, yellow-flowering herbs, like

[12] Ritter, C. (2016). *Heilpflanzen Signatur und Botschaft: Zeichensprache der Natur erkennen und nutzen* [*Healing plants – Signature and message: Recognising and using nature's sign language*]. Stuttgart: Ulmer Verlag, p. 89

St. John's Wort often represent a sunny disposition, mood-lifting. They give a warming, positive feeling. If St. John's Wort often catches my eye, if I find it particularly beautiful, perhaps it is related to what I am currently lacking or what would do me good.[13] So, with this in mind, we can learn a lot from plants and learn something about ourselves by looking at plants. Basically, it is no different from asking ourselves why a certain person impresses or negatively agitates us. Oftentimes, this feeling tells us much more about ourselves than it does about the other person.

[13] ibid., pp. 53–55

<u>L</u>: I would like to hear more about that. You say: "When I'm out with people", or that you're "out for a walk". Why are we going out?

<u>M</u>: Adventure pedagogue Peter Becker says: "On the quiet, adventurous being on the way becomes a school of the senses and a laboratory of feelings in which there is no generalization but in which attention is directed precisely to the otherness and particularity of nature. They prevent the senses and the feelings from becoming dull."[14] 'Being on the way'[15], you cannot perceive and take in everything. You don't have a focus on every detail in your surroundings, otherwise you probably wouldn't be getting anywhere and be completely overstimulated. You have to put on filters to be able to be on the way. But something always draws your attention and that's the exciting thing you should pursue to find out why that is. In opposition to that, in rooms and in the house, you're not exposed to the many stimuli of being on the move and you're consciously influencing your environment.

[14] Becker, P. (2012). *Wind lispelt, biegt Bäume und macht frösteln, Wasser gluckst, spiegelt und erfrischt. Zur Notwendigkeit einer sinnorientierten Bildung* [Wind whispers, bends trees and makes us shiver, water gurgles, reflects and refreshes. On the necessity of a sensory-oriented education], p. 41, translation: Lea Maria Spahn

[15] 'Being on the way' is a term in adventure-based pedagogy that describes (semi-structured) journeys which are centered around individual or group experience. They are encounters with oneself and the other in a very fundamental sense.

<u>L</u>: If you could formulate how people can get in touch with their plant environment – perhaps we could say it already starts with breathing or, as you say, we go for a walk and we notice certain things – how would you formulate suggestions as a wild plant educator or human-plant mediator? How would you capture "Walking as Embodied World-making" from your perspective? Being on the move seems to be a central mode for you, after all?

<u>M</u>: While being on the way, we can experience states of musing or get into flow states which change perception as we get into walking, moving, looking around on our path, but also drifting off with our thoughts. Or we get to know different seasons, see plants change and transform throughout the year – much more than we humans or animals do. This is also a recommendation or almost a wish of mine, to pay close attention. Perhaps even to go on your favorite walking routes in the park or forest and observe the plants also in the course of the year. To find out and experience in which atmospheres they grow, with which plants in neighborhood, in which symbiosis, how the plant looks in different months, how healthy it looks. With these questions, our view becomes more holistic and instead of a momentary discovery, a more comprehensive encounter. There are other beautiful nature coaching approaches. In guided plant

encounters, for example, one stays with a plant for a while and enters into an intuitive exchange with it. You observe how the atmosphere affects you, try to ask questions to the plant, aloud or silently in your thoughts, and use techniques from meditation practices. There are also some interesting observations and reports that people have similar experiences, that seemingly some plants trigger similar moods, states of mind, sensations. The presence of a birch tree triggers different sensations than a large, powerful oak tree. This is very exciting. You can try this form of encountering plants simply by pausing and staying with a plant while being on the way.

> L: I have taken a few walks several times this year to see changes: What is growing, what is dying, what is growing into each other? But also, to see that some plants become invisible or I suddenly became aware that trees, for example, have usually been in one place much longer than I have. This aspect of different lifetimes or temporalities is fascinating.

M: With trees, it's very obvious – the lifespan. However, even in this case, we oftentimes have a limited and anthropocentric view of plants. The plant is not always dead when it fades in the fall or winter. Many of them are perennial. If we would change our perspective in this regard, the existence and unique temporality of plants could be perceived quite differently.

> L: Also, their mode of existence can confront us with questions about what we perceive or don't perceive, what happens without our influence or even goes unnoticed. What have you learned from and through plants as fellow living beings?

M: Especially the aspect, that I can learn a lot about myself through plants, by always being open to perceive what plants trigger in me and questioning what issues could be behind that. That was a very fascinating approach for me. And what I still find very impressive is to get to know new plants every month, every year, or to rediscover already familiar ones. When I give a seminar for instance, of course, I take a look at the places that I will be facilitating. And usually something catches my attention. This is how I always discover plants that I don't know yet or know far too little about. I research whether the plant is edible, if it has certain healing powers, if I can make color from it, or which myths and legends are known about it. Depending on the goal with which I am walking around, I first look for specific plants and yet I constantly discover new ones and learn. That's what fascinates me – and what I love about my work.

> L: What is it actually like to go into an encounter with plants, not walking past them but including them into the way we move through the world?

M: Taking the point of view of plants is to understand plants as a very essential part of our world, also as a life form that made life on earth possible for us humans and animals in the first place. It's trying to take off the anthropocentric glasses for a completely new view of the world. To question what we believe to be a given and to open ourselves for something new. Exactly this, the opening for the new, is a very essential aspect of being on the way. So, opening up and looking at what life, growth, movement or reproduction looks like in the plant world will in turn open completely new dimensions of experience for us. To dive into the diversity of plants and their being in the world unlocks a whole new wisdom for me which changes my view of the world. This is exactly what many botanists are working on, such as already mentioned Stefano Mancuso or indigenous botanist Robin Wall Kimmerer.[16] She is an American plant ecologist at State University of New York and professor at the College of Environmental Sciences and Forestry in Syracuse. As an author, she combines her perspectives as a scientist and as a Member of the Citizen Potawatomi Nation and has set herself the task to combine traditional ecological knowledge of the indigenous peoples with environmental science. Not only that, she passes this wonderful attitude on to her students as well as to the readership through her books. A lot of her work is about gratitude, connectedness, and an attitude towards plants. A particularly nice impulse is her appeal to choose the language more consciously and to allow the plants a vitality, a "personality".[17]

[16] Kimmerer, R. W. (2013). *Braiding sweetgrass: Indigenous wisdom, scientific knowledge, and the teachings of plants.* Minneapolis: Milkweed Editions

[17] Kimmerer, R. W. (2021). *Zwei Essays: Die Grammatik der Lebendigkeit* [*Two essays: The grammar of aliveness*]. Berlin: 42 w_orten & meer

L: What changes as a result of taking the perspective of plants, engaging with them in this way, and allowing this mode of perception to emerge?

M: When I'm walking, I observe how the atmosphere of my surroundings and the mood within me changes, my fellow world influences me. We can all notice an atmospheric difference when we imagine hiking or walking in a deciduous forest or in a purely coniferous forest – the mood is quite different, isn't it? But how about training the perception to notice also single plants on our way and what moods they trigger in us, how they influence the atmosphere of the place, of the space in which we move.

L: As a very last question, what else would you like to share that is important to you or that you see as a principle of your work?

M: My wish is that we humans get rid of our biased and 'superior' view of plants and move through the world with an openness; that we try to take off filters and get involved in plant encounters.

Lea Maria Spahn
Posthuman Bodyscapes – Walking in the Czech-German Borderland

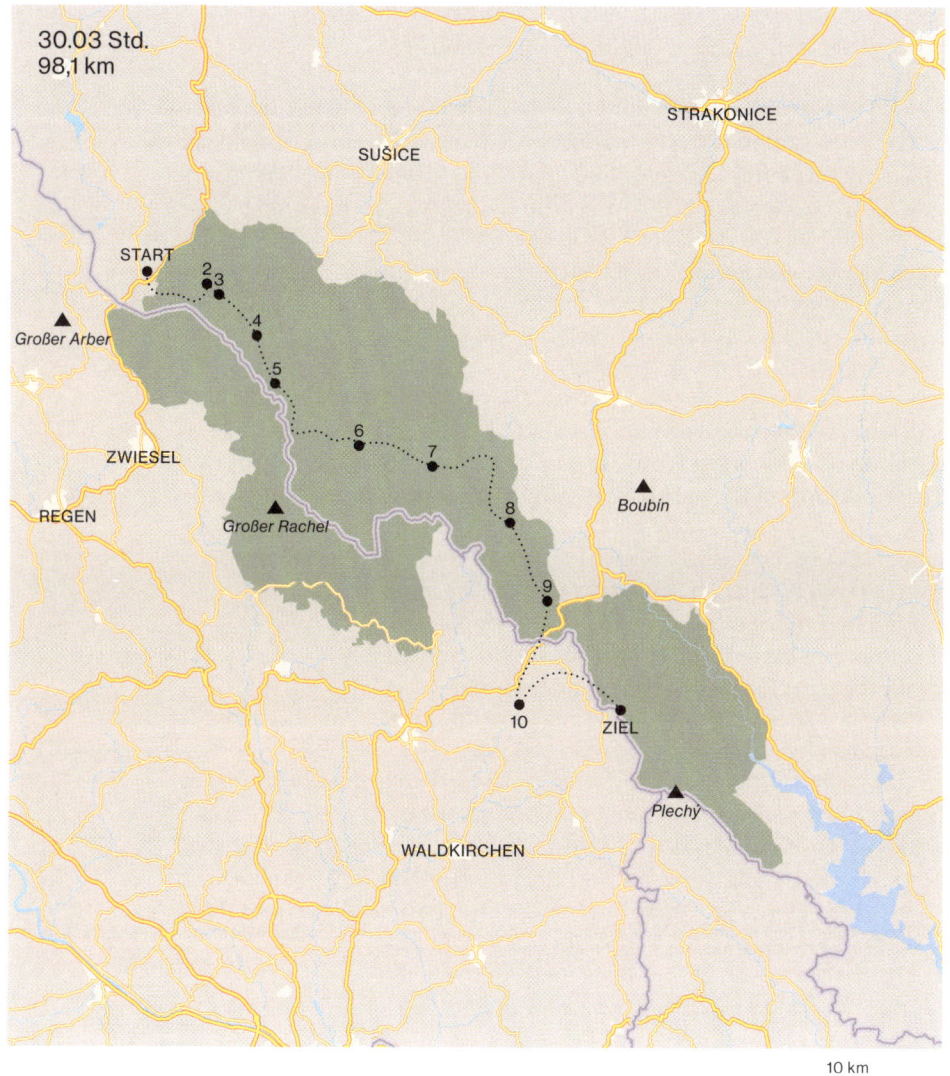

This article reflects a 10-day symposium in the form of a hike through the Czech-German national park Šumava. The symposium was organized by the Agronauts*Collective, a Czech-German collective that addresses the intersection of aesthetic practice, performative research, and environmental activism. With 'crossing borders' as its principle, the process-oriented work can be situated within posthuman epistemologies as a laboratory for "multispecies becoming-with to cultivate the capacity to respond, response-abiltiy".[1] Facing the challenges of anthropogenic interventions and the necessity of planetary politics, the article elaborates on the potential of walking as methodology for a posthuman phenomenological research. The walking journey will be framed through the notion of *bodyscapes* to address the question of how bodies can be conceptualized as entangled materialities and part of multi-species ecologies in becoming.

[1] Haraway, D. J. (2016). *Staying with the trouble: Making kin in the Chthulucene.* Durham: Duke University Press, p. 78

ENTERING THE PROJECT: THE AGRONAUTS*JOURNEY
IN THE CZECH-GERMAN BORDERLAND

The Agronauts*Journey took place in the Czech-German borderland in September 2020. With its starting point on the border between Bayrisch Eisenstein/Železná Ruda, the participants entered the national park and walked from emergency camp to emergency camp over the course of 10 days to reach the camp site in Nové Udolí as final destination. The project consisted of 12 invited researchers and artists from Czech, Germany and France from the fields of performance theory and dance, theatre, environmental sciences, psychology, outdoor education, fine arts, and sociology of movement.[2]

The concept was based on walking in the Czech-German borderland which is historically marked by the 'iron curtain' that cut through this landscape to demarcate the division between West-Germany and the Soviet Union until 1989 – and still carries traces of the political division and border regime. Today, this border zone is part of the "green belt" of Europe, a transnational nature preservation area and a space of political remembrance.[3] For the journey, the participants arrived with their backpacks, tents, sleeping bags and individual 'research interests'; two more participants and a car were also part of the journey supporting the group with the transportation of belongings, food and water wherever possible – they were an important moving infrastructure of care.

The project itself was based on the fictional character of the Agronaut* that had emerged in a previous project which sparked questions of artistic practice and environmental activism. In this article, I will concentrate on the way that this character allowed to re-imagine bodies – the Agronaut* elicited imaginations of "a body's could-have-been and might-become; it is [...] potentiality from which bodies are selected and actualized".[4] The Agronauts*Journey is situated within the tension field of lived bodies – the body-bound subjectivities – and a relational becoming in multi-species environments. As a consequence, this article is written from a post-phenomenological perspective which is interested in the experience of being a body and its relation to the world as *situated* sensory and subjective experience. It highlights that the lived experience is situated within social and material contexts and as such differentiates our 'being in the world' critically – not as a universally given experience but one that has to be reflected from an intersectional perspective taking into account the incorporation and felt experience of power structures and social inequality. As embodied beings, we are radically bound to the lived body, the 'zero point' of existence, as it is formulated by phenomenologists.[5] The lived body is materially given as it is the foundation of our situated encounters with the world from *here*. But as sensory and material organism, it is also always entangled with its environments. And this became apparent through the walk, through the responsiveness of our bodies-in-movement. Due to the pandemic situation, we had decided to stay a long stretch of

2
The participants had applied with a personal 'project interest' and were between 25 and 35 years old.

3
URL: https://www.european-greenbelt.org/; https://www.icomos.de/icomos/pdf/eiserner-vorhang-undgruenes-band-iron-curtainand-green-belt.pdf

4
Neimanis, A. (2017). *Bodies of water: Posthuman feminist phenomenology.* London: Bloomsbury, p. 47

5
There is a broad body of research concerned with the phenomenon of being; for an overview see:

Zahavi, D. (Ed.). (2012). *The Oxford handbook of contemporary phenomenology.* Oxford: Oxford University Press;

Alloa, E., Bedorf, T., Grüny, C., & Klass, T. N. (Eds.) (2019). *Leiblichkeit: Geschichte und Aktualität eines Konzepts* [*Embodiment: History and relevance of a concept*] (2nd ed.). Tübingen: UTB;

for a feminist re-reading see: Landweer, H., & Marczinski, I. (2016). *Dem Erleben auf der Spur: Feminismus und die Philosophie des Leibes* [*Tracing experience: Feminism and the philosophy of the body*]. Bielefeld: transcript

time in Czech Republic so we would not have to cross borders as often. We oriented ourselves according to the online map we had developed using the detailed color-coded paths in the park area. The shared document provided a navigational tool, but the experience was more paced by the daily walking through and in a landscape. The constant 'being-on-the-way' was an influential force and can even be considered a facilitator of the journey.

WALKING AS METHODOLOGY FOR MULTI-SPECIES ENCOUNTERS

Walking is an immersive experience of the lived body as and within a passage through environments over a span of time. Traversing the national park was a performative journey based on the somatosensory experience of the moving body in space.[6] Reflecting the journey, walking becomes apparent as an embodied practice of somatosensory encounters and open experimentation based on posthumanist phenomenology[7] – as a way to co-create new imaginaries and bodily sensibilizations in multi-species worlds.[8]

From this perspective, walking is an embodied and responsive movement based on proprioceptive and sensory impressions: Step by step, relations of proximity and distance change; step by step, the body is the vehicle of encounter: noticing, observing, feeling, smelling, touching and being touched, approaching and leaving behind, orienting according to hiking signs, finding one's rhythm, following another person, listening, feeling the tiredness etc. At the same time, as a posthuman phenomenology would argue, walking is a movement practice within complex socio-material conditions and horizons that I will capture through the notion of *bodyscapes*.

The journey unfolded as moment to moment walking encounter while also being structured by aesthetic research practices and ongoing collective practices of care like meal preparations, eating, constructing the tents every day anew. Another influential force were the changing weather conditions that affected the packing and walking. Noticeably, these practices all had the same importance for the project's process. For example, in the beginning, building the tents was a rather long process of scanning a place for finding a good spot, learning how to build the construction and moving in with the mats, sleeping bags and backpacks. After some days, building the tents became a routine: The eyes knowingly searched the ground for a suitable spot and the appropriate distance to trees; the construction turned into co-working that needed little words, the materials were known, and the tent seemed an embodied spatial experience.[9] These practices were as much knowledge-generating as were the aesthetic and reflective practices that differentiated our experience of and responsiveness to that environment. For example, we went into long phases of sensory exploration in different parts of the landscape that allowed to focus on a small part of ground and its life. Or we stood in a long line on an outlook and played with the eye's searching of the horizon by focusing on different layers of it. Or we met with a forester of the national park who took us on a walk off the paths to introduce us to forest areas as complex adaptive ecosystems characterized by

[6] Paterson, M., & Dodge, M. (Eds.). (2016). *Touching space, placing touch* (1st ed.). London: Routledge

[7] Neimanis, 2017

[8] Neimanis, A., Åsberg, C., & Hedrén, J. (2015). Four problems, four directions for environmental humanities: Toward critical posthumanities for the Anthropocene. *Ethics and the Environment, 20*(1), 67–97

[9] See also Susanne Nemmertz in this book.

"dispersed interaction; absence of a global controller; cross-cutting hierarchical organization; continual adaption, perpetual novelty; far-from-equilibrium dynamics".[10] This also mirrors a shift in thinking about futures, namely, to acknowledge what is not known and evades predictability.[11] Stress factors such as parasites or climate changes need synthesizing research and observations with regard to the interdependence of socio-economic and environmental systems.[12]

As such, the aesthetic research practices that shaped the journey were framed by questions like: Could the notion of the Agronaut* spark research practices that perceive and attend to post-human entanglements? How could the walking journey as durational exposure to this environment render trans-corporeal entanglements tangible? And could the practices be translated into an ethic of care?

BODYSCAPES – OR MULTI-SPECIES BECOMING

"[P]osthuman feminism provides understandings of bodies as operating simultaneously across different interpermeating registers, from the biological or chemical to the technological, social, political, and ethical."[13]

The narrative of the journey changed through these shared experiences and reflections – within the aesthetic practices, by meeting with local actors, but also by being on the way as a group. For instance, in regard to the paces of walking: Often, the group that set off in the morning would stretch apart as participants decided to follow their own walking rhythm as backpacked body. For some participants, the slowness exalted the perceiving of a surrounding, a space became less a landscape to be traversed but an atmospheric multitude that the moving body became part of. Attending to the sight of moss, the changing sounds over the course of a day, or the textures of different grounds, all the somatosensorial perceptions were a relational becoming, a shift in sensory responsivity in which the lived body reverberated in the echo of its encounters. As we were crossing through landscapes, exposed to weather, environmental, atmospheric conditions, the 'we' became a relational and processual (im)possibility – ever re-configuring: "The ways in which we understand what it means to be a body, the cartographies that our bodies chart, and our inextricability from complex webs of relations are all lived by us, in phenomenologically relevant ways".[14] This quote by Astrida Neimanis amplifies 'being a body' as lived experience through her conception of a multimodal and posthuman embodiment.[15] Consequently, she speaks of a "dispersed embodiment"[16] sensitive to the interrelatedness of felt sensations in their implicatedness. Neimanis unfolds that in her work on 'Bodies of Water' in which she lays out how watery flows connect across times and spaces as materializations of socio-ecological, historical, and power relations. In her work, the term 'posthuman' refers to the implicatedness of the social; the implicated subject is considered a relational becoming within socio-material

[10] Nocentini, S. (2011). The forest as a complex biological system: Theoretical and practical consequences. *L'Italia Forestale e Montana*, 66(3), 191–196

[11] ibid., p. 193

[12] This is captured by Haraway's term of 'nature-cultures' as described in f.n. 20

[13] Neimanis, 2017, p. 23

[14] ibid., p. 58

[15] Phenomenological methodologies start from embodied experience of perception, the 'being in the world' as living (human) body (esp. Maurice Merleau-Ponty); A posthuman phenomenology expands the anthropocentric understanding of embodiment to introduce the notion of 'more-than-human' as locus of research in its dynamic force of entangled and implicated becoming as Stacey Alaimo or as Stacey Alaimo, Astrida Neimanis and others argue.

[16] Neimanis, 2017, p. 26

constellations. This material entanglement, this 'being part of' environments also generates an understanding of material relations with/in lived bodies as „responsive ethico-politics"[17] – and with that, Neimanis suggests a radical shift in our understanding of politics towards a responsive and ethical involvement: "If phenomenology asks us to understand the world as lived, we can only begin from a situated politics of location – albeit one whose spatiotemporal scale is torqued through posthuman relationalities and becomings."[18] Against this backdrop, I will develop the notion of *'bodyscapes'* that conceives of bodies as becoming in a multi-species world.

This line of thinking accentuates, that the sensory openness *'towards the world'*[19] renders bodies responsive to their surroundings but more so, that these bodies are also (made) *'of this world'*, as Donna Haraway argues.[20] Taking this as conceptual starting point of a posthuman becoming, the research journey can be outlined as a process of becoming sensitive to our *'being-of-the-world'* by being exposed to a specific environment and learning about it in the process of walking (in) it. Human bodies are "always more-than-coherent, bounded, subjects"[21], they are more-than-human. To be more-than-human is the foundation of an embodied research practice that relies on the vulnerability of organisms and the intra-connectedness of systems in their socio-historical and entangled becoming.

How does this relate to the walking journey? The walking was the durational exploration of the processes of interdependent worldmaking as naturecultures[22], a research process, and a practice of critique. This posthuman understanding of bodies allows to conceive of the breathing, walking, sensing body as part of and within its non-human co-agents and environments as intra-active worlding.[23]

Being on the way, we introduced experiential aesthetic entry points as invitations for the day's walks. Quietly listening, finding one's rhythm, playing with horizons of seeing, or place-making were interweaving interventions while moving within and among this forested environment. As an example, "slug time" emerged as a temporal measurement by closely observing the ever-expanding movement of a slug on a path. The observation turned into a moment of sharing time and twisted perceptions: Which creature was crossing? Did we cross its path or did it cross ours? How do we become sensitive to the travelling or migration movements of other species? At another time, one of the participants took a rest on a rotting tree stem. Sitting and resting, the silence was broken by a dead tree falling with sharp, cracking sounds. He became the witness to this moment of falling after an unknown lifespan. This could be interpreted further with Ladino's reference to tone as "affective relay"[24] between selves, things and an environments in which this relay takes place; it is an encompassing affective relation in which affective atmospheres are co-created. It was moments

17 ibid., p. 26

18 ibid., p. 25

19 Merleau-Ponty, M. (2002 [1945]). *Phenomenology of perception.* London: Routledge

20 Haraway, 2016, where she describes human and non-human beings as being "of the world as its storied and dynamic substance, not in the world as a container", ibid., p. 91

21 Neimanis, 2017, p. 47

22 Haraway, D. J. (2003). *The companion species manifesto: Dogs, people, and significant otherness.* Chicago: Prickly Paradigm Press. This notion examines the entanglement of the concepts of 'nature' and 'culture' in constellations of ecological processes, technological artefacts, and more-than-human actors e.g. in the field of political ecologies and theories of the non-dual, see: Gesing, F., Knecht, M., Flitner, M., & Amelang, K. (Eds.). (2017). *NaturenKulturen: Denkräume und Werkzeuge für neue politische Ökologien* [*NatureCultures: Thinking spaces and tools for new political ecologies*]. Bielefeld: transcript

23 Barad, K. (2003). Posthumanist performativity: Toward an understanding of how matter comes to matter. *Journal of Women in Culture and Society, 28*(3), 802–831. URL: https://www.journals.uchicago.edu/doi/full/10.1086/345321; see also Shira Wachsmann in this book

24 Ladino, J. K. (2015). Mountains, monuments, and other matter: Environmental affects at Manzanar. *Environmental Humanities, 6*(1), 131–157

like this, responding and listening to experiences that gave rise to a sensibilization for relational entanglements that constitute a posthuman becoming. As Haraway formulates: "Maybe, but only maybe, and only with intense commitment and collaborative work and play with other earthlings, flourishing for rich multispecies assemblages that include human people will be possible".[25] Translated to our walking practice, this meant staying in a rhythm of moving through a landscape, being exposed to and enveloped by shifts in perception that emerged from that. The walking provoked a sensibilization and differentiation of embodied perception; being a body shifted to being *bodyscapes* in spatio-material, atmospherical and somasensory entanglements.

The notion of *bodyscapes* resists visible differences and boundaries for a focus on entangled materializations and temporalities. In applying this term, the journey spawned dispersed and transversal connections as foundation for a posthuman phenomenology of becoming in a multi-species world.[26]

Following these posthuman trajectories, the journey meant to be among non-human beings in multiple, existentially dynamic and continuous encounters. Researching this entangled 'being-of' is embedded in a multispecies ethnography that nevertheless relies on the somatosensorial apparatus of perceiving bodies. Traversing and being with this biosphere reserve and national park, the living and lived bodies became medium and subjects of research – as much a sensitive and sensate organism as a vulnerable and porous assemblage in becoming. This ambiguity of 'the human body' is addressed especially by new materialist perspectives that stress that we have never been only human.[27] Rather, they stress the trans-corporeal entanglements of ecological, technological, socio-political, and other systems in a mutual becoming at different scales.[28] In that way, *bodyscapes* highlights trans-corporeal realities by walking through and within the Czech-German borderland. The walking journey shed light on the entanglement with environments and their im/material traces.

RE/FORMATION OF BODIES AS BECOMING

"(W)e need to devise new social, ethical and discursive schemes of subject formation to match the profound transformations we are undergoing. […] The posthuman condition urges us to think critically and creatively about who and what we are actually in the process of becoming."[29]

Based on this perception of *bodyscapes*, I want to elaborate on the relation to the specific landscape we were tranversing. Following Jones, landscapes are a "becoming-in-place […] a hyper-complex interplay of practice, time, space, memory, text/image and materiality, all of which is compressed through the extraordinarily rich, ongoing moment of affective becoming".[30] What this perspective on landscapes highlights is not only the encounter as performative presence that encompasses

[25] Haraway, 2018, p. 81

[26] However, a posthuman approach cannot stay indifferent to socially constructed and lived power relations that materialize as embodied subjectivities. It has to register situated and specific differences and analytically define entities across, through and within the body/scapes it examines.

[27] Haraway, D. J. (1991). *Simians, cyborgs, and women: The reinvention of nature.* New York: Routledge; Braidotti, R. (2001). *Metamorphoses: Towards a materialist theory of becoming.* Cambridge: Polity Press

[28] n S. Alaimo & S. Hekman (Eds.), *Material feminisms.* Bloomington: Indiana University Press, 237–264

[29] Braidotti, R. (2013). *The posthuman.* Cambridge: Polity, p. 12, where she advocates 'affirmative' politics that combines critique and creativity; in her conception, posthuman subjectivities are "materialist and vitalist, embodied and embedded, firmly located somewhere", ibid., p. 51

[30] Jones, O. (2015). Not promising a landfall: An autotopographical account of loss of place, memory and landscape. *Environmental Humanities, 6*(1), 1–27, p. 4

different materialities in their becoming, she also regards this encounter as constituted by memory. She stresses the "lived geographies of remembering and forgetting"[31] – which became very present throughout the journey as the vast national park is still bearing traces of the 'iron curtain' borderline from decades ago. In addition to that, science art projects are "ongoing performance of memory"[32] that enter, question, touch, and shape epistemic terrains. Art science activism deals with living on a damaged planet. In this way, the walking journey can be seen as a worlding, a "'making with'[...] proper to complex, dynamic, responsive, situated, historical systems".[33]

As a consequence, 'becoming' signifies an active presence shaped by intra-acting material and memory traces that constitute the present: The journey was influenced by history/stories on the way: Meeting a Czech ranger who gave us information on the military presence and other interventions in the national park during the time of the 'iron curtain'. He also pointed out that the core zone of the park is understood as 'laboratory of nature itself' where the logic of forest management is not applied. Meeting a German tour guide, we learned about the forced resettlements when the area was military borderland and a zone of refugee passages. Also by sharing and listening to our differing national perspectives on historical events in their particularity and partiality – all of the histories/stories that shaped the journey worked as entangled affective forces that touched us as moving *bodyscapes*. By being touched, the "echoes of the stories"[34] influenced our journey. They initiated narrative re-configurations that we collaboratively weaved into our passage; the exposure to the echoing stories and somatosensory experiences yielded a becoming-with: The remembered, sensed, and perceived matters were included in the *bodyscapes* as affective atmospheric body-land-scapes. While Ladino reminds us that all landscapes are processive and dynamic, it is this realization of *'being-of-the-world'* that made our entanglement palpable. Different agential (human and non-human) materialities and affective forces collaborate in this process of becoming. It is the specific intra-active dynamics in the meeting of temporalities, rhythms, and sensualities that converge as socio-historical and material traces. The posthuman phenomenological approach attends to these transcorporal scapes as "eco-affective entanglements".[35] Yet, the human body as experiential and situated medium remains of importance. The encounters of bodies and specific landscapes entail an ambiguous becoming.

31 ibid., p.4 – Here Jones delineates how she seeks "to express differing inflections on how displacement can affect presence-absence and how it can manifest itself in landscapes, and be bound up with powerfully lived geographies of remembering and forgetting, 'ecologies of place' and mappings of melancholia".

32 Haraway, 2016, p. 69

33 ibid., p. 25

34 Ladino, 2015, p. 150

35 ibid., p. 155

WHAT IS LEFT: COMPOSTING THE PROJECT[36]

While walking, the physical, lived and living bodies are junction points of im/material impressions and stories – and our (socio-historically mediated) orientations towards the world.[37] This marks an interesting point in our research process: Our bodies arrived into the project as (already) sedimented histories and subjectivities. At the same time, the journey unfolded as a spatio-temporal entanglement of these

36 Composting is here taken up from Haraway, D. J. (2015). Anthropocene, Capitalocene, Plantationocene, Chthulucene: Making kin. *Environmental Humanities*, 6(1), 159–165

37 Ahmed, S. (2006). *Queer phenomenology: Orientations, objects, others*. Durham: Duke University Press

Landscape close to Poledník, Czech Republic

bodies and a specific landscape.[38] As entangled situation, the body can be regarded as "lived spatiality, oriented to a situation wherein the lived/living/lively body embarks on an architectural dance that actively spatializes (and temporalizes) through its movements, activities, and gestures [...] and it continuously reconfigures its own corporeal schema in responding to and recomposing its milieu (Umwelt)". [39] This statement highlights the reconfigurations of the corporeal schema through the exposure to and entanglement within the journey. The notion of *bodyscapes* is therefore one way of capturing the intra-active re-configuration of the walking bodies over the course of the journey: the somatosensory impressions are to be understood as responsive echoes travelling across bodies, the group body and the environmental milieu as "affective assemblage".[40]

How was that experienced during the journey one might ask? On our journey, we crossed through a vast area of dead sprouces that towered in the landscape as remains of a bark beetle infestation. What at first was experienced as a looming atmosphere of a once living forest area, turned into a lesson of understanding a landscape anew: Instead of 'managing' this strip of landscape from a forestry perspective, the national park administration's response had been to 'allow nature to be nature'. By not intervening and managing, the landscape became a research laboratory on a more-than-human scale. The slow decomposing of trees was visible as it also showed an eco-system's intricate connectivity: the fallen tree trunks were the hotspots for seeds to sprout into new trees. This clash of temporalities became a lesson as our impression of loss was transformed into another understanding of the entangled dynamics of microbial activities in the decomposition process as well as its functioning as habitat for a diverse range of plants and animals. Our first – very human – response was shaken, our first re-actions so short of understanding the entangled ecosystems we are a part. Walking was way of mapping these relational (epistemic) territories following but also creating lived maps of the National Park. This article has outlined a posthuman phenomenological research approach that attends to the intra-connectedness of bodies-in-becoming.

As a conclusion, the Agronauts*Journey turned out to be a frame for experiencing how landscapes in the Anthropocene are storied and, undoubtedly, shaped by human practices; they are "assemblages of organic species and of abiotic actors [that] make history, the evolutionary kind and the other kinds".[41] To inquire into these assemblages means, as Haraway points out, to enter into an interlacing ongoingness thick with dis/continuities. Research methodologies dealing with this interlacing of the biological-cultural-political-technological share the critical reflection of human hegemony and the imagination of research as kin-making.[42] *Bodyscapes* then turn out to be collectives of kins in their mattering – biologically, historically, semiotically, and intra-actively. Going back to the first entry point of the Agronauts*Journey, walking as means of research starts from and twists conceptions of the corporeal presence of researchers. Entering the landscape of the borderland thus meant to create research practices that both acknowledged the embodied relations and committed to being part of multi-species

38 'Composting the project' here refers to Hamilton and Neimanis' sharp reflection on the influence of feminist theory and theorist for environmental humanities: "to notice not only what is being transmogrified, but also under what conditions, why, and to what effect", see Hamilton, J. M., & Neimanis, A. (2018). Composting feminisms and environmental humanities. *Environmental Humanities*, 10(2), 501–527

39 Coole, D. (2010). The inertia of matter and the generativity of flesh. In D. Coole & S. Frost (Eds.), *New materialisms: Ontology, agency, and politics.* Durham: Duke University Press, 92–115

40 Ladino, 2015, p. 152

41 Haraway, 2015, p. 160

42 ibid., p. 161

assemblages. The Agronauts*Journey can issue attentiveness to an ethical dimension of research practices while attending to environmental and political questions. In this way, the notion of *bodyscapes* is "not about right responsibility to a radically exterior/ized other, but about responsibility and accountability for the lively relationalities of becoming of which we are a part".[43]

[43] Barad, K. (2007). Meeting the universe halfway: Quantum physics and the entanglement of matter and meaning. Durham: Duke University Press, p. 393

National Park Šumava/Böhmerwald, Czech-German borderland

Astrid Lembcke-Thiel
Footnotes

Curatorial footnote

These pictures are actually inconsequential. They are spontaneous collections of impressions that I captured with my cell phone, because they make my here and now visible while walking. They are tiny snippets of my perception while I am in motion. An attempt to connect myself with my surroundings, my wonder, my irritations, and my being in the world. I am the place of collection of these impressions.

Diese Bilder sind eigentlich belanglos. Es sind spontane Sammlungen von Eindrücken, die ich mit meinem Handy eingefangen habe, weil sie mein Hier und Jetzt im Gehen sichtbar machen. Es sind winzige Schnipsel meiner Wahrnehmung, während ich in Bewegung bin. Ein Versuch, mich selbst mit meiner Umgebung, meinem Staunen, meinen Irritationen und meinem in der Welt sein zu verbinden. Ich bin der Ort der Sammlung dieser Eindrücke.

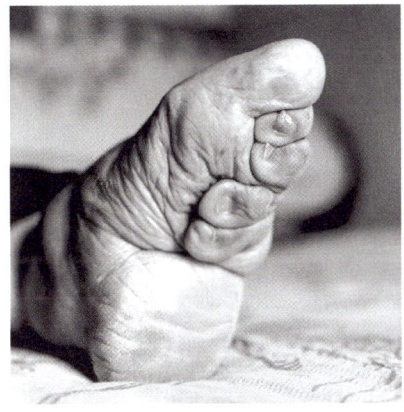

How did I become who I am now?
What has my body experienced?
How much did I have to bend, curve, fold, compact...

...to grow up within (my) limitations?

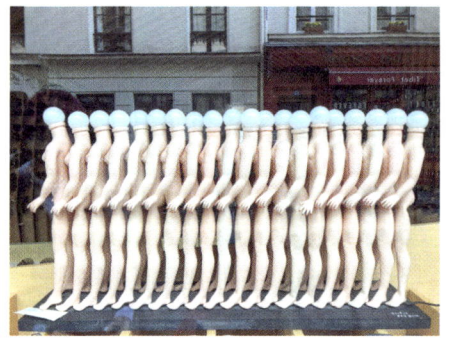

Irritations have frightened me.

 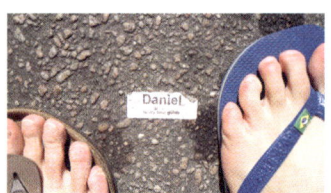

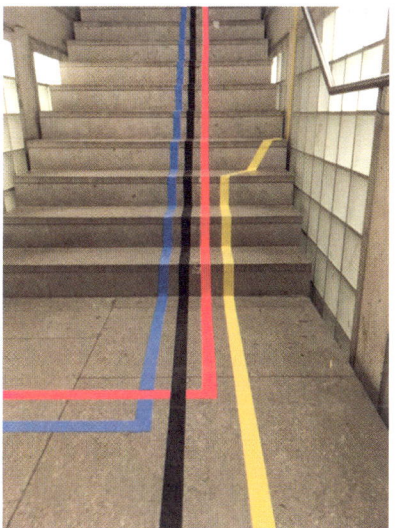

Multiple impressions challenge my learned, habitual systems of order.

How many unsettling experiences do I gather and endure
in order to locate myself?

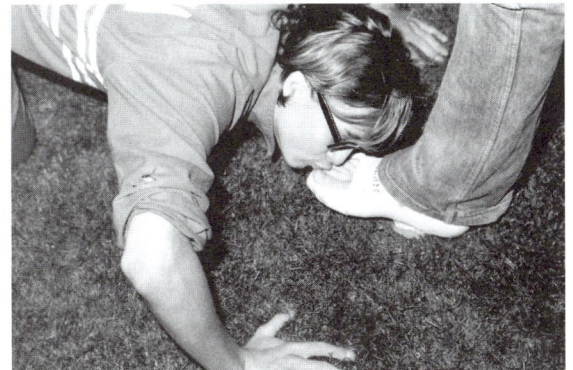

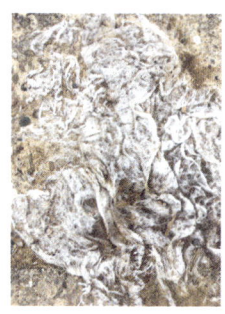

What kind of detours do I take?

What do I discover
in my environment
that I do not understand,
that I cannot decipher?

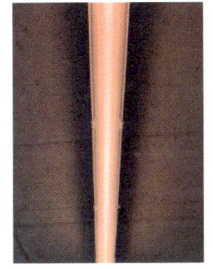

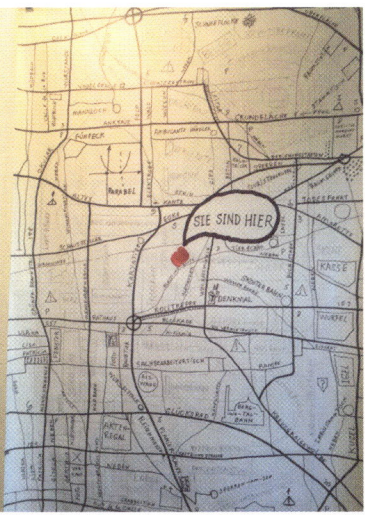

Some is painful, some is easy, wondrous, illogical, violent, frightening, alienating. I record everything in my body archive. My coordinate system of perception continuously stores all information between above and below, inside and outside, forward and backward, between becoming and passing away.

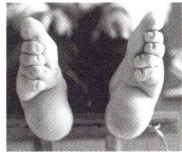

2nd Part

Walking in the (Performative) Arts

Antonín Brinda
East by Northeast: (Dis)Obedient Walking, (Dis)Obedient Riding

KICK-OFF

In the following paper, I am diving into my artistic research[1] *East by Northeast*, a project that I conducted under the framework of the Live Art and Performance Studies at the Theatre Academy of the University of the Arts, Helsinki, Finland.[2] The main (impossible) goal/research question was finding ways how to articulate, how to perform (mega)cities through the movement of the body through their transportation networks. I have worked *with* and *within* the (mega)cities of Moscow (Russia), Ulaanbaatar (Mongolia), and Beijing (China).[3]

There are many differences between the three selected cities but also several important similarities. They are all interconnected by the Trans-Siberian Railway, the longest passenger transportation network of its kind on Earth. They are all capitals, core cities in which the need for both efficient urban planning and control over the movement of crowds are very high. All share a socialist past and all were strongly influenced by Soviet urban planning. Finally, all are currently experiencing impacts of a certain kind of free-market economics. In each of the cities, I stayed for approximately one month.

The issues of global mobility and tourism were some of the important motives for the research: Why, where, and how do people travel and what are the factors influencing their mobility? What is my position as a white European male researcher-tourist in the context of global travel and how can I move around the world in a non-exploitative, non-offensive, environmentally justifiable way? Apart from trying to find new ways of how to perform (mega)cities, these issues were appearing and disappearing throughout the project and as background of this article.

In this paper, I would like to introduce some of the key aspects of the methodological approach I was using within the respective three cities. With minor adjustments, it could be applied to various urban environments. I will begin by introducing two theoretical terms: Wolfgang Schivelbush's *machine ensemble* and *fictional order* derived from Michel de Certeau's thinking. Both of the concepts are an important part of the methodology – the former as an inspirational, navigational tool that was often in the back of my mind, the latter as a backbone of the research. In the second part, I will discuss specific examples of my performances from Moscow, Ulaanbaatar, and Beijing and offer an in-depth insight into the experience of performing (mega)cities.

[1] Brinda, A. (2019). *East by northeast or performing the (mega) city: Movement of a body through transportation networks.* Helsinki: TEAK

[2] The written part of the diploma work dealt mainly with my final artistic research East by Northeast that I conducted across two continents, took me several months, and involved dozens of people. The project consisted of photos, videos, audio, writings, maps, performances, discussions, presentations, artist talks, and one workshop. Selected documentation from the project can be accessed here: antoninbrinda.com/about-2/

[3] An important moment of the research was also a presentation of selected material in the form of an exhibition in the Space For Free Arts (Vapaan Taiteen Tila) in Helsinki in June 2018. Documentation of the exhibition is accessible here: antoninbrinda.com/exhibition/

I

MACHINE ENSEMBLE

One of the starting points of the project was the relation between intra- and intercity transportation, more specifically, the phenomena of the railway and the various political/social/economic transformations its invention brought.

A great source of inspiration was the work of culturologist and historian Wolfgang Schivelbusch who brought my attention to a specific cyborg[4] unity between a traveler and the means of transport, especially the railway.

The starting point of his *machine ensemble* concept is a report from 1846 on the railway construction in which one can read that "the wheels, rails, and carriages are only parts of one great machine"[5], that the entire railway could be perceived as a single entity. Schivelbusch adds that this organism includes the whole "unified railway system, which appear[s] as one great machine covering the land".[6]

He speaks about the machine ensemble in a strictly technical sense as about a compound of different mechanical components. The traveler participates but is not unified with the machine.[7] Taking this further, I propose an expanded, cyborgian understanding of the term that incorporates also the human elements. One of the essential functions of mechanical components is to interact, collaborate, with human ones. Though, there are obvious differences in the nature of the organic and inorganic parts of such a railway machine ensemble. One of them is the ability of people to disconnect, to leave the railway system.

Who is in power in this organic-inorganic ensemble? Is the train being operated by the human driver or the driver being used by the train? The question applies to various means of transportation but is especially significant in the case of the railway,[8] "because a train runs on a predetermined line an engine-driver could never aspire to the social role of a 'captain on dry land': The electric telegraph confirmed his true status, that of an industrial worker, an operator of a machine".[9] Similarly, who is in charge of the passenger-train ensemble is not as clear as it might seem.

The railway is a service enabling transportation of humans but allows itself to be used only under certain specific conditions: "To get in, as always, there was a price to be paid".[10] But not only in a sense of money: "Inside [of the train carriage] there is the immobility of an order",[11] writes French philosopher Michel de Certeau, "[i]mmobile inside the train, seeing immobile things slip by".[12] Onboard of any means of transportation, the passenger is always more or less restricted. If one is not driving a vehicle such as a car or a bike that enables the individual to stop as they please passengers are being temporarily imprisoned by the machine.[13]

PERFORMING THE FICTIONAL ORDER

An even more expanded notion of the machine ensemble could consider *cities* as one such interconnected organism. There are also some similar tensions between a city apparatus and its users as between vehicles and their operators/users.

[4] I understand the term "cyborg" in its common meaning – i.e. "(in science fiction stories) a creature that is part human, part machine", Oxford Learner's Dictionaries, www.oxfordlearnersdictionaries.com/definition/american_english/cyborg,

[5] Greenhow, C. H. (1846). In W. Schivelbusch (1986), *The railway journey: The industrialization of time and space in the 19th century.* Berkeley & Los Angeles: University of California Press, p. 40

[6] Schivelbusch, W. (1986). *The railway journey: The industrialization of time and space in the 19th century.* Berkeley & Los Angeles: University of California Press, p. 47

[7] For example: "machine ensemble [...] interjected itself between the traveler and the landscape. The traveler perceived the landscape as it was filtered through the machine ensemble." (ibid., p. 189, italics added)

[8] As it is with subways, tramways, trolleybuses, and the like machines in which the individual vehicles are inextricably connected to the united machine ensemble network.

[9] ibid.

[10] de Certeau, M. (1984). *The practice of everyday life.* Berkeley: University of California Press, p. 113

[11] ibid., p. 111

[12] ibid.

[13] With various notable exceptions such as when driving a car on a high-speed highway where to entirely stop the vehicle is hardly possible.

In his seminal work, *The Practice of Everyday Life*, de Certeau discusses the conflict between pedestrians and cities. He compares the relation between walking and urban environments to that of a speech act and language, of a system and its actualization.[14] As for users of a language, also the freedom of walkers is limited, possible only within the constraints of the given urban system. But that does not mean that city users have no agency. Quite the contrary – according to de Certeau, they develop everyday individual "tactics" through which they resist the order imposed on them from above by "strategies" of a "subject of will and power (a proprietor, an enterprise, a city, a scientific institution)".[15] Through their 'erroneous' behavior, pedestrians discover "their own paths in the jungle of functionalist rationality".[16]

Consider, for example, the phenomenon of the desired path, a human or non-human-made pathway created by walking within or outside an urban environment. While the urban design prescribes for walking sidewalks and streets, spontaneous creators of desired paths break such order by choosing ways that feel more intuitive, more practical.[17]

The image below displays a slightly absurd conflict between the governors of an (unknown) park and its users. The desired path originally made as a creative response to pavements built by the city is here 'made inaccessible'. Not able to acknowledge its fictional nature, the city tries to restore order:

14 ibid, p. 97

15 ibid, p. xix

16 ibid, p. xviii

17 Such freedom to create an own pathway has, nevertheless, its limitations. I.e. it might not be possible to cross a busy street or a highway at other places than the prescribed ones.

A city tries to block access to the desired path

Similar to other urban inhabitants, I was experimenting with the disciplinary spaces of cities – just more consciously and analytically. Unlike some other artists, I was not trying to find new and unusual strategies on how to 'hack' the city. Instead of searching for new pathways, new 'words' how to 'speak' a city through its transportation networks, I decided to articulate its 'grammar' as precisely as possible. Not being a rebel but, quite on the contrary, being the most passionate follower of the system, the ideal user, worshipping the geometries, the timetables, the tracks, etc. *ad nauseam*. And by that, actually being a rebel because, if the order of things within the city is fictional, its rigorous following could be seen as inappropriate, subversive.

As a comparison, consider the work of Tehching Hsieh, *One Year Performance 1980-1981 (Time Clock Piece)*, in which he "punched a time clock every hour on the hour" for one year, recording the "breakdowns" in which he failed to do so; to assure the legitimacy of the project, "to avoid any suspicion of cheating", he issued several binding contracts, signed either by himself or by an invited witness.[18] In this piece, Hsieh, like me, became a worshipper of an order and a perfect worker, although absolutely useless. Despite the resemblance to the activity of factory workers, after one year of punching the clock, Hsieh did not produce anything 'useful'.

Such an approach, which might be described as 'maximum effort – minimum result', is a strong message in our contemporary world obsessed with efficiency and (over)production. By his words: "I'm not doing object style art but I like thinking. I'm working hard but I'm doing almost nothing. That's the way I like it".[19] The nine to five working routine or our division of time into 'minutes', 'hours', or 'years' is as much a fiction as the urban order. Both Hsieh's and my work address this fictionality.

The combination of the two concepts – that of a *machine ensemble* and a *fictional order* – impacted the way I was articulating the chosen (mega)cities. The notion of *machine ensemble* made me realize that humans in cities are partly in charge, partly subjugated, operating while being operated. The *fictional order* became the power structure to be explored and challenged from the mentioned perspectives. The following section gives three practical examples, one from each researched (mega)city, providing an insight into the articulations that occurred.

II

PERFORMING THE THIRD RING ROAD (WALKING)[20]
18.–19. March 2018, Moscow, Russia

The transport infrastructure of Moscow is defined by its target-like shape. I was intrigued by the city's circularity and decided to articulate it mostly through its orbital roads and highways.[21] See the map of Moscow:

18
Hsieh, T. (1980). *One year performance 1980–1981*. Tehching Hsieh website: https://www.tehchinghsieh.net/oneyearperformance1980–1981

19
Hsieh, Tehching (2017), in: Delaney, Brigid: Tehching Hsieh, extreme performance artist: ‚I give you clues to the crime', www.theguardian.com/artanddesign/2017/oct/24/tehching-hsieh-extreme-performance-artist-i-give-you-clues-to-the, accessed 6th December 2021

20
The audio diary from the Third Ring Road walk can be accessed via the following links:

18. 3. 2018 I soundcloud.com/east-northeast/18-3-2018-moscow/s-SgZz8
18. 3. 2018 II soundcloud.com/east-northeast/18-3-2018-ii-moscow/s-K7xB6
19. 3. 2018 I soundcloud.com/east-northeast/19-3-2018-moscow/s-ypmpC
19. 3. 2018 II soundcloud.com/east-northeast/19-3-2018-ii-moscow/s-VRqZx
For the video excerpt from the performance please refer to this link: youtu.be/mLstt4UOqhY

21
Read more about Moscow and its urban structure in Brinda, op.cit. 1, p. 133, and about the notion of circularity in my research on p. 129

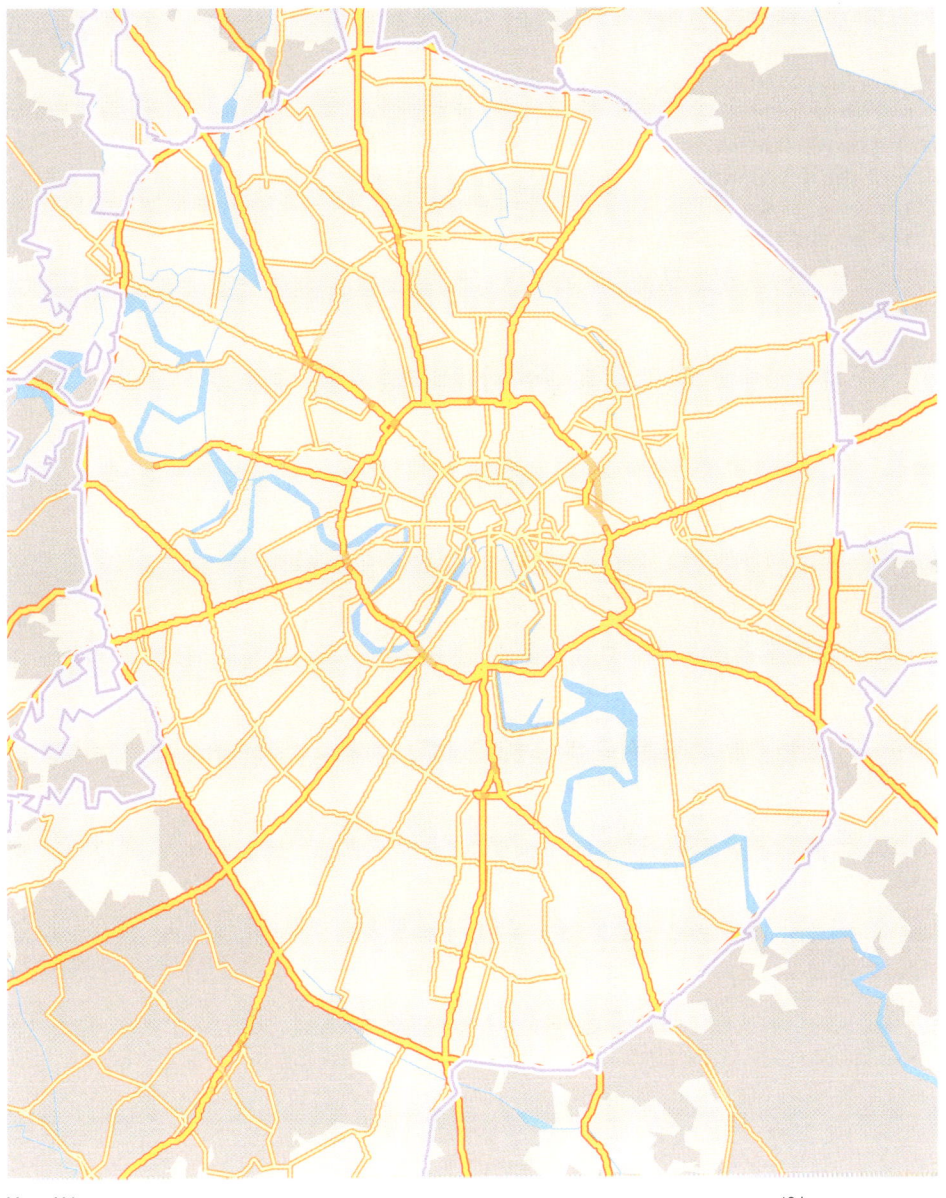

Map of Moscow 10 km

The walking performance *Performing the Third Ring Road (walking)* was the longest one in a series of similar articulations.[22] In this action, I walked around the Third Ring Road (Tretye Transportnoye Kolco, TTC) – a 35 km-long orbital highway. The origins of the Ring dates back to the Moscow 1935 General Plan[23] with construction beginning in 1960. It was fully completed only in 2005. This one was the longest of Moscow's ring roads which I could walk on taking into account the scale and conditions of my research.

22 ibid., p. 135

23 Chernishev, S. E., & Semenov, V. N. (1935). Генеральный план реконструкции города Москвы / General'nyĭ plan rekonstruktsii goroda Moskvy [General plan for the reconstruction of the city of Moscow]. Landscape-Design website: https://www.landscape-design.ru/articlex.php?c=Moscow-reconstruction-1935

The ring is dedicated mostly to cars. There is no public transport service operating all the way around. There is often no official pathway for pedestrians and, in segments, the beltway also disappears in tunnels under the ground. Urban geographer Robert Argenbright calls the TTC a "state-sponsored obsession with the automobile"[24], pointing out its negative impact on the appearance of the city and the environment. According to him, the TTC "reduces the amount of public space available" and "endangers civil society".[25] From this perspective, my walk could be seen symbolically, as a march for healthier/more pedestrian-oriented cities.

Performing the Third Ring Road (walking) took two full days. I tried to stay as close to the beltway as possible but in many cases, I had to make detours. At times, I lost the highway and had to search for it again. In other cases, the corridor for pedestrians got so narrow that to walk on it next to several lanes of non-stopping traffic was possible but just felt absurd. Although, sometimes I encountered fellow pedestrians even in the most unpleasant sections of the road.

I did not want to interrupt the walk and the consistency of the performance. For that purpose, I found myself a hostel located next to the TTC, where I spent the night after the first day of walking. It was a strange feeling to pay extra money for lodging in a shabby hostel (as ordered by the project budget) located not more than 20 minutes metro ride from my usual accommodation. If one is used to traveling by public transport, especially by the metro running in the darkness of the underground, it may be difficult to acknowledge the actual distances within the city. Often walking from one part of a big city to another might be comparable to a day or several days long trek.

During my walk, I observed the diverse environments of the city from unusual perspectives. I saw brownfields, the International Business Center, garages and high-rises, construction sites, trains, and shopping malls; I walked on rails, through a cemetery, next to the stream, on bridges and under them, and much more. To be able to imagine my walk better, see several selected photographs of the highway surroundings:

[24] Argenbright, R. (2003). Making space for the new middle class: Moscow's third transport ring. *Osteuropa, 58*(4–5), 1386–1399

[25] ibid.

Images 1–6: Peforming the Third Ring Road (walking)

6

As already mentioned, the walk might be perceived as a call for change, addressing an ecological cause. More importantly, it was just what it was – a performance (in a sense of doing, operating) of a human particle of a much bigger machine ensemble. I meticulously followed the prescribed pathway but the whole activity was – from the perspective of the city-machine (or capitalist society) – unproductive, irrational. I was also on the wrong path, so to say, as the road was not intended for pedestrians which made the march even more absurd. As if I was a cogwheel inserted in a wrong part of a machine – running precisely but unnecessarily.

THE BUS IS THE TRAIN (OR PERFORMING CANCELED INTRAURBAN TRAIN CONNECTION) (BUS+WALKING)[26]
17 April 2018, Ulaanbaatar, Mongolia

While the infrastructure in Moscow and Beijing is expansive and efficient[27], the capital of Mongolia, Ulaanbaatar, only dreams about such efficiency. In Ulaanbaatar, I worked within the existing transportation network but focused on the articulation of the city's dreams, of how it wants to be developed, how it wants to perform (in a sense to appear, to present) itself. It wishes not to be seen as dysfunctional and backward but as a modern city, a capital interconnected with the rest of the world through a new international airport and on the intracity level operating smoothly with its BRT[28] lanes and the new underground system.

The following paragraphs discuss an articulation of one of Ulaanbaatar's dreams: the (closed) sub-urban rail line. Take a look at the linear shape of the city located in a valley on the Tuul River:

[26] The video documentation of the performance can be accessed here: youtu.be/elggiqG_zCY

[27] The subway systems of the two megacities are very reliable and efficient, but the public transport on the ground is subject to the same heavy congestions as personal cars.

[28] Bus Rapid Transport – This form of urban transport is common in cities of developing countries (i.e. Bangkok, Istanbul, Beijing, Jakarta). One of its main features are lines of traffic dedicated for the BRT buses only or an off-board fare collection.

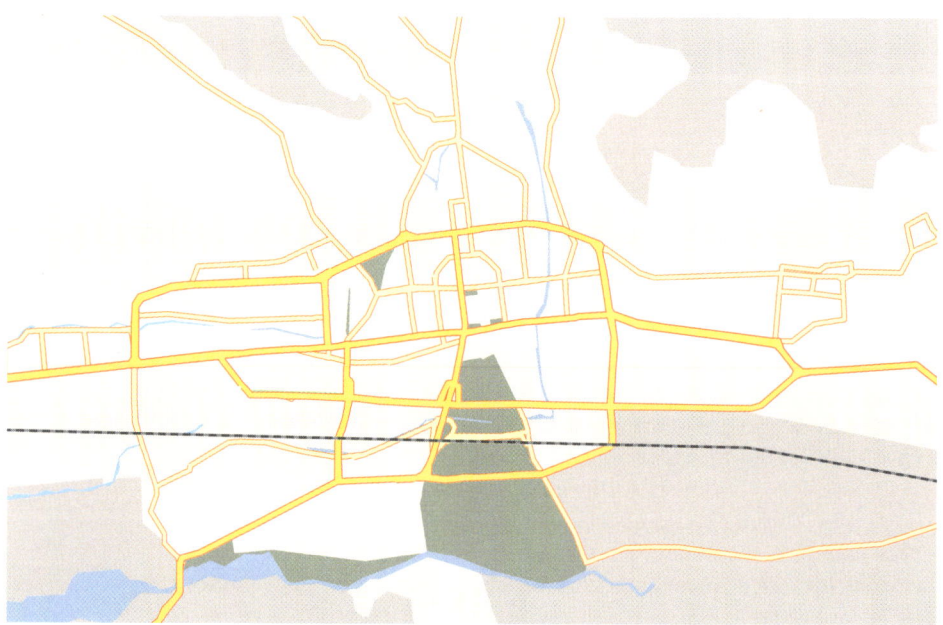

Map of Ulaanbaatar

As can be seen on the map, there is a horizontal railway line running through Ulaanbaatar. The rail is the city's main orientation vector together with its main boulevard, Peace Avenue. During the time of my visit, the trains running on the line were mostly carrying cargo while, less frequently, there were some transporting passengers across Mongolia and internationally. In 2014, the line served as a so much-needed suburban connection for commuters with its railbus train.[29] But the project did not prove to be sustainable and was canceled.[30]

For *The Bus Is the Train (or Performing canceled intraurban train connection) (bus+walking)*, I decided to explore how could I substitute the closed connection and designed for myself an alternative route by public buses. See below the path I have taken. The grey color marks the closed commuter line:

[29] NewsMN (2014). City railbus in service from today. News.mn website: https://news.mn/en/181420

[30] Manusov, V. Z., Bumtsend, U., & Demin, Yu. V. (2018). Analysis of the power quality impact in power supply system of urban railway passenger transportation – the city of Ulaanbaatar. *IOP Conference Series: Earth and Environmental Science*, p. 177

Ulaanbaatar 17. 4. 2018

To imagine the atmosphere of Ulaanbaatar better, see a selection of photos taken during one of my other walks in the city on April 7 as I do not have photo documentation from *the performance*. Notice the new blockhouse buildings being constructed rather uncontrollably around the city, contrasting with traditional ger[31] houses and the environment in the background:

[31] Ger is a Mongolian equivalent of a yurt, a portable, circular dwelling made of wood, felt, skin. While gers have been part of the traditional Mongolian nomadic culture, they are nowadays also being used as permanent housing in cities. The bigger half of Ulaanbaatar's population lives in gers. (The World Bank Group (2018): Better Air Quality in Ulaanbaatar Begins in Ger Areas, The World Bank website: www.worldbank.org/en/news/feature/2018/06/26/better-air-quality-in-ulaanbaatar-begins-in-ger-areas,

7

8

Images 7–10: Performing Chinggis Ave –
Worker's St – Ard Ayush Ave –
Tasgan Rd – Ikh Toiruu – Ikh Khuree
(walking) [32]

For this paper, I decided to focus on an articulation of Ulaanbaatar that explores a more significant urban pattern and issue than the articulation from which I am displaying the photos. Yet the walk around the city in Performing Chinggis Ave – Worker's St – Ard Ayush Ave – Tasgan Rd – Ikh Toiruu – Ikh Khuree (walking) had also its qualities. Contemporary Ulaanbaatar is defined by its linearity but its core has been designed in a circular (resp. rectangular) way by Soviet planners following the pattern of Soviet cities (Byambadorj – Amati – Ruming 2011, p. 171). Circling around Ulaanbaatar provided me with a valuable overview of the city's current state. I could witness the uncoordinated construction of housing blocks in the inner periphery, ger settlements mostly outside the ring, mountains limiting the growth of the city on the north and south as well as factory districts and fading parks for recreation covered in the ever-present dust.

For the beginning and end of my substitute ride, I chose the train stations in the city suburbs: Amgalan (in the East, where I have begun) and Tolgoit (in the West, where I have finished). These are also the two stations between which the canceled railbus operated.³³ For a foreigner, it is not at all easy to get oriented in the bus schedules of Ulaanbaatar. Not only was it difficult for me to find the way from Amgalan to Tolgoit but evenly challenging was to discover how to get from my home to the two peripheral areas and back.

The travel from one side of the city to the other took me around one hour and forty minutes. In Moscow or Beijing that would not be anything strange but in a significantly smaller Ulaanbaatar, this is a very long duration taking into account the distance traveled (some 20km). But maybe I was still lucky considering that (as the data from 2011 show) the travel speed of bus traffic in Ulaanbaatar can drop to 5–8 km/h during peak hours.³⁴

At one point in the travel, I had to switch buses and to arrive at my transfer station I had to walk through a ger area. Corrugated iron fences, dust, unpaved roads, stray dogs, a half-dried stream, people pushing trolleys with water canisters, no street or direction signs – that was for me the atmosphere of the unexpectedly visited ger district. When using public transportation in Ulaanbaatar, instead of a smooth transfer, the experience is confusing, challenging, and in cases brings one into the labyrinthine neighborhoods where the presence of foreigners might not be very appreciated.

My experiments in the city of Ulaanbaatar lead me to the conclusion that its machine ensemble is quite a dysfunctional one. It wants to be but is not yet a powerful "unified [...] system, which appear[s] as one great machine covering the land".³⁵ The city wishes to establish an order of functionality but that ambition is largely unrealized. Its "strategies", in de Certeau's sense, remain 'truly' fictional.³⁶ Though I kept my "tactics" of obedience and rigor, the context was different.³⁷ In Moscow, I encountered the city's fictional but apparently confident and proud order. In Ulaanbaatar, I was acting more like a henchman – a person who anticipates and hopes for a transfer of power and from the shadows expresses his support for the future autocrat. I entered the realm of wishful fantasy and dreamed Ulaanbaatar's dream.

33 News.MN, op. cit. 8

34 Tsevegjav, N. (2014). *Urban transport system in Ulaanbaatar city*. United Nations ESCAP website: https://www.unescap.org/sites/default/files/4b.2_UT%20System_Ulaanbaatar.pdf

35 Schivelbusch, 1986, p. 47

36 de Certeau, 1984, p. xix

37 ibid.

PERFORMING JING-JIN-JI (TRAIN)
16–17 May 2018 Beijing, Tianjin, Xiong'an (Baiyangdian)

Let me open up the final section by presenting the map of the last researched city – Beijing. Although, this time, I am showing it more just *pro forma* because the artwork I am about to discuss dealt with a machine ensemble bigger than Beijing.

Performing Jing-Jin-Ji (train) was my key articulation in China. It resembles many of my Ulaanbaatar articulations as it focuses on the infrastructure that is yet to be created. One of the important differences between the two contexts is the probability of completion. Various parts of the Jing-Jin-Ji project in China are in constant development. The same can not be said about the modernization plans of Ulaanbaatar.

Jing-Jin-Ji is supposed to be, or from today's perspective (2022) it, perhaps, already is, what some call a "supercity"[38] or a "megaregion"[39]. The shortcut stands for Beijing, nearby megacity Tianjin and the surrounding province of Hebei. The goal of the project is to interconnect the three places into one giant urban environment with over 100 million inhabitants.[40] One of the project's aims is to boost the region's economy. There are also other advantages Jing-Jin-Ji hopes to deliver. Decentralization of services should alleviate some of the most pressing of Beijing's maladies such as overpopulation, pollution, traffic jams, or water shortages.

[38] Johnson, I. (2015). As Beijing becomes a supercity, the rapid growth brings pain. *The New York Times* website: https://www.nytimes.com/2015/07/20/world/asia/in-china-a-supercity-rises-around-beijing.html

[39] Shepard, W. (2016). China commits $36 billion to further build the 110 million person Jing-Jin-Ji megaregion. *Forbes* website: https://www.forbes.com/sites/wadeshepard/2016/12/08/chinas-110-million-person-jingjin-ji-megaregion-gets-a-new-36-billion-railway-plan

[40] The inspiration can be found in similar agglomeration developments in South China such as the Yangtze River Delta and the Pearl River Delta.

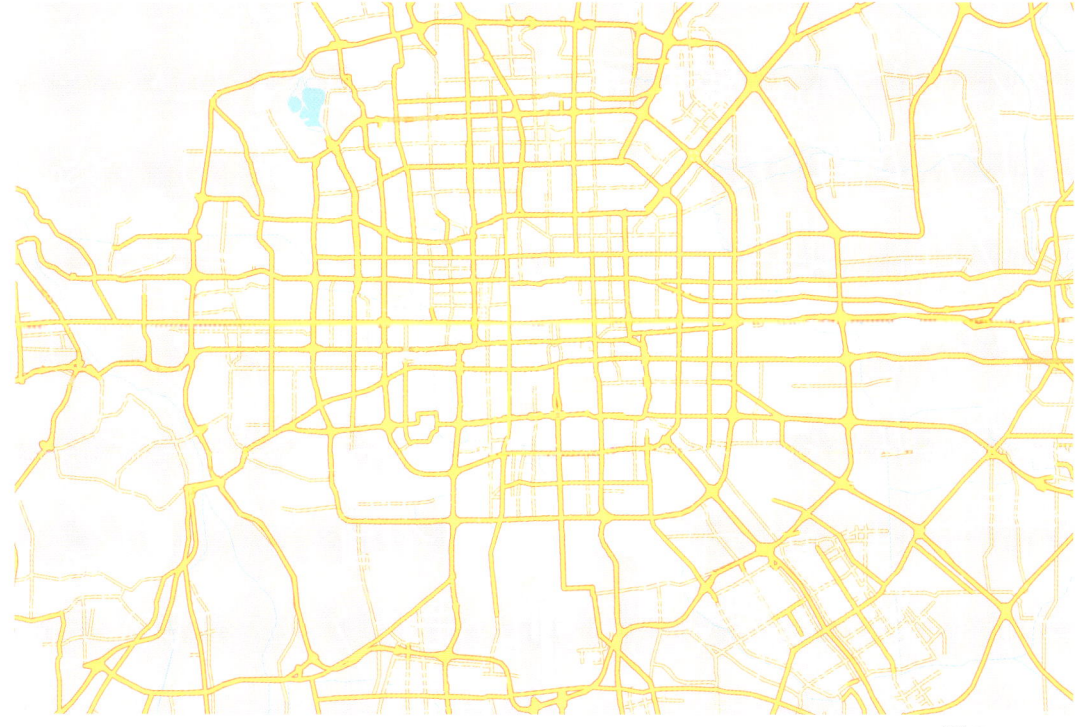

Map of Beijing

For an urbanized territory of this scale, a high level of interconnectivity is essential. That is why new highways are being constructed, as well as high-speed railways and even a brand new airport.[41]

In my articulation of the growing megaregion, I decided to travel from Beijing to Tianjin, from Tianjin to the Xiong'an New Area, which is one of the key developing sites in Hebei province, and back to Beijing. I have chosen to use (high speed) trains which shall soon become a crucial means of transportation for the region. I divided the trip into two days. At first, I stayed in and explored Tianjin, an important Chinese port city of 14 million. The second day, I continued to Xiong'an. See the map displaying my trip below:

[41] Beijing Daxing International Airport opened in September 2019. This and Beijing Capital International Airport are China's most important international airports. *Deutsche Welle* website: https://www.dw.com/en/beijings-huge-new-daxing-airport-opened-by-xijinping/a-50573170; Preen, M. (2018)

16: Performing Jing-Jin-Ji (train)

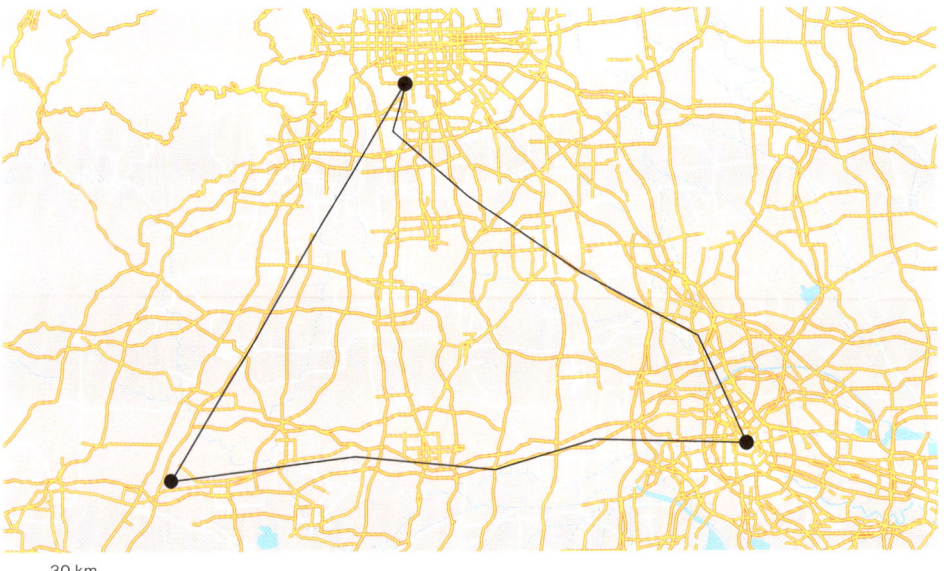

30 km

While the travel to Tianjin was – relatively – easy, to get to (and from) Xiong'an was quite a different story. I arrived by train in a nearby city called Baiyangdian and walked several kilometers from the station to the city center. Unable to find other means of transport in Baiyangdian, I eventually decided to use the services of an auto-rickshaw taxi – a shaky small vehicle on three wheels.

At my final destination, I expected to encounter a land devastated by rapid urban construction. But to my big surprise, I arrived at the entrance of a water amusement park. Instead of skyscrapers, I ended up observing Chinese tourists chewing on ice lollies and enjoying rides on boats. Throughout my whole trip, I did not encounter any visible signs of the coming megaproject other than a (closed) office in Baiyangdian with a sign "ENN Coordination Services Center Of Xiongan New Area" on its facade. At least this was evidence that I was not in a totally wrong place. My return was not very smooth either and I ended up, for the first and last time in China, hitchhiking back to Baiyangdian train station.

See the video still displaying a peaceful Lake Baiyangdian:

17: Lake Baiyangdian

On the two photographs below, compare the difference in atmosphere between the megacity of Tianjin and the significantly smaller city of Baiyangdian:

images 18–19: Tianjin and Baiyangdian

To open up the work a bit, I would like to briefly discuss the last common performance of Marina Abramović and Ulay: *The Lovers* (1988). The notorious three months-long march from the opposite ends of the Great Wall of China was originally supposed to be an act of an ultimate connection between the two lovers. After meeting each other in the middle, they were supposed to get married. But over the eight years, when they negotiated the permission from the Chinese government, that idea shifted from marrying to breakup. And as the story goes, this is also what happened.

Through their walk, the wall became the third entity involved in their relationship to which they wanted to give an epic ending. As they marched on the leftovers of once a solid, magnificent structure, they were likely evaluating the fading of their common narrative, an intense 12 years work, and love affair. This powerful performative gesture marked the end of one period in their lives and the beginning of a new one.

In *Performing Jing-Jin-Ji (train)*, I was articulating the future expansion of the megaregion through the movement of my body, thinking about its past and present, and how the upcoming development could change it. As in *The Lovers*, I was performing a shift from one state of being to another. The performance of Abramović and Ulay was direct, crucial for their personal life and their performative gesture had an immediate impact. My trip was more abstract, not playing such an important role in my personal life and my gesture did not have the same power to alter reality. But through my presence, I was announcing, anteceding, the physical realization of other performative proclamations. Their authors will be Chinese authorities responsible for the new infrastructural developments in the area.

Once again, I became the most passionate "servant of the city, a realizer of its desires"[43], although as passionate as being also its critic. The piece could be seen as a commemoration of the soon-to-be-lost environment, an articulation of a path that maybe should not be taken. The new constructions will bring development but also a more structured environment more subjected to power. Through my incapacity to travel to the 'glorious' Xiong'an, I celebrated the opposite of what China is so proud of: The dysfunctional interconnectivity and the related decrease in control of individuals.

[43] Brinda, 2019, p. 149

FAREWELL

I tried to present the key principles of my methodology utilized in the *East by Northeast* project. Throughout the research, I encountered different machine ensembles within which the fictional order functioned in diverse ways. I explored environments that usurped their fictional power (Moscow), dreamt about its consolidation (Ulaanbaatar), or were actively working on its expansion (Beijing).

This research wants to be a playful but rigorous take on the issue of urban planning, introducing new perspectives on how to see our (mega)cities. If I had chosen different walks and rides the narrative details of this paper might differ, and yet, the resulting overall message would remain the same. The articulations of the established, dreamt, expanding, or other kinds of fictional orders of cities give insight into the ways these urban environments are structured, the ways people and other entities use them and are being used by them. The project provides a critical perspective on the power-ridden logic behind the transport infrastructure and unveils the societal norms associated with the notion of 'functionality'.

My way of working in the *East by Northeast* project related to various other phenomena that were only indicated in this paper – the Trans-Siberian railway, the (post)socialist urbanism, the figure of a tourist, etc. But the core methods are transferable, and I invite and encourage you to try them out:

Identify and follow the key patterns of a city. Articulate them. Enter the machine ensemble. Become slaves. Become masters.

ANa Anaa
Bodies of Transit

There have been moments I recall as transformative because they let me reach intense emotional states and shift from one to another merging also memories of places. That is probably where *bodies of transit* originates from, even though the precise location will always exist as a mirroring of territories of experiences in or about to be transferred.

I remembered that I had seen these fences before,

Somewhere else, but not *here*.

Standing aside, one beyond another, as duplicas. The signalisation at each gate "no entrance to visitors", "no public allowed" linked to an aggressive horizontal and vertical bordering generated an impenetrable zone. The very dry ground, led to a flashback of the walls keeping apart Mexico from California.

> It was more like an emotion. Not feeling at the right place, not belonging there, hostile realms to anyone who did not have a *pass* to cross over. I faced the priviledge which goes with *whiteness*. I had been told before I left: You will see what freedom of movement means. My German passport let me through, in any direction, back and forth. *From where does back and forth even start or end? Which directions does it imply?* We were not from *there* but had inherited the right to go through. To be let through.

Here, I stand now on the other side, outside of the fence, actually between. I took roads and crossroads leading to a place where you are free to go but cannot go in.

It is a very loud surrounding, a place obsessed with movement. Trucks driving fast, charging the air with dust and disappearing in each other's sounds. A continuous coming and going. Sometimes they loose part of their loading on the way when they engage in a turn. Machines in motion, to be heard beyond fences and walls. Large scale structures breathing in and out.

I wondered how I could engage with these creatures.

As far as I could go, the site's expansion itself is limited by the blue line of the ocean. Exactly at this threshold is a huge recycling site dealing with waste from the whole surrounding industries and the city itself. I stood *t/here* watching these metallic arms frenetically rotating, picking meticuloulsy the right amount of trash to gently drop it on treadmills going upwards which forward it to a black hole that swallows it *all*. Trucks feed this tongue all day long. What is hunger to a machine which is conditionned to express the need to ingest?

I stood there for a while captivated by this being.

I then kept going on along overgrown sideways. The shiny surface of a plastic sheet caught my eye. It seemed large enough to cover half of my body. I began to use it as a *sun-screen*, a slight shade that gave me some rest. After a while, I needed to change the steady position of my arms. My fingers were sweating by being in touch with the plastic under this heat. I stopped and looked around.

    I was not meant to be *t/here*.

    The term of *living* has to be reviewed: *T/here, it is mainly mechanically animated*. These roads are paths to industrialized lands, to the left overs of such industries. How can *territories* be impregnated by production sites? By which means do infrastructures withhold information? While going *back* I follow a road leading along warehouses without windows, which seem to continuously breathe. Exhaling a smell which expands over a mile around. It is half sweet, the other half is pure disturbance of the senses. It is almost frightenly revulsive.

Walking becomes emotionaly charged with exhaustion. Imagination unfolds in worst case scenarios or contemplation of perfectly organised structures. Workers were rotating on site during maintenance walks, gathering, smoking after lunchbreak on stairs wearing outfits specific to each workplace. In a twisted turning movement assimiliating one to another and in the meantime separating one from another.

May this be a comment on walking, opening a discussion of bodies of transit.

My presence on the polder was initiated by taking part in a five-day workshop by Elvia Teotski[1] for the master students in fine arts of EESAB in Brest. She intended to introduce us to a research on embodied practices of walking linked to particular territories. She wished us to go through these industrial realms, to move along traffic roads, to have no shelter, to feel the summer heat, and our bodies consuming liters of water. What is and becomes a body in a place which is drastically affecting its bare existence? What can we *take* from there? Which emotions can we transpose/transfer? She wanted us to deliberately cross through this area, to get lost *t/here*. Which paths would we follow? Could/would we endlessly wander without final point to reach?

[1] www.elviateotski.com

I did the same path four times for two hours each and slightly changed the time of departure. I wanted to walk again and again on the same road, merging the memories of each one of the walks.

As participants of the seminar, we impregnated an indoor space by our continous coming and going over the course of the week. On the last day, we shared our investigations in this room we thought to inhabit as a collective gathering of what we had experienced – the emotions, smells, trash we had found. Imagine a subtle suspension and floatingness of colors and textures. May you feel there our exhaustion of days spent going back and forth.

I had intended to mirror, reincarnate, this transcending state of containing and being contained, diving into the performativity of belonging/s. At what state am I possessed, do I feel possessed, or do I possess? More than possession, I wanted to get rid of its meaning implying domination. Containing is holding, is being hold, wrapping carefully. May it be inside you.

Do you remember what you have absorbed this morning before leaving? Was it a fluid or solid entity you had to swallow? Do you remember each sip? Was it warm? Were you in a hurry or did you let the flavours and textures impregnate you? Has this influenced your emotional state of the day? Did it become yours instantly? Or each time you eat/drink, do you refer to this *other* you need to sustain yourself? Does it feel like ingesting something external to you? Where have you taken it? Where are you *now*? Where is *t/here*? Have you assimilated this *other* presence? *Have you become this other presence? Or do you still feel it moving through you?*

I (lost) track (of) memories.

I am, became we, them, they; we were, are, will be, shifting, endlessly transforming beings, rehearsing aliveness in our deepest womb. Take it as an invitation, a meditation, to generate layers of timeframes slightly deviating one from another. Conveying presences held within, demultiplying when ever you let them exist inside you. They might never be fully yours, existing on their own. Being *one another.*

I have to admit that I came to write about food and wombs because they are somehow places which are emotionnaly charged and affected. By walks, by landscapes I pass through, by the speed of my walk, the slowness of certain mornings I wake up with an overwhelming hunger, not necessarily driven by a need to ingest someting but, as I could call it, by being a body of transit seeking for care. _When are you fully aware that you are never one but rely on a surrounding and embrace this state of tremendous coexistence?_ May then be our quest to not rush, to not instantly fill a gap, an amount of missing energy by food or coffeine but to encounter this excitement and dive into the realm of the body as territory. Feeling these landscapes of emotions, tensions, calls. To wisely decide what I swallow, and wonder, if then comes release, if then I move differently.

I feel that anything I ingest[2] pulsates inside me and deeply influences on how I percieve my surroundings and, furthermore, engange with my proprioception.

[2] From the verb ingérer, which means ingesting, absorbing. It necessarely refers to the internal activity of a body.

Take it from there with PCB (polychlorinated biphenyls) [3] and the gentle suffocating, mutations we cannot avoid. I *demand* you to listen to these inner Voids/Voices. Loud. Screaming, scattered frequences to act acording to the thresholds they open up. Embracing posthumanism. We enter the realm of altered flesh. Altered movement. How does walking in toxic realms open us to these encounters? May these grounds be anywhere, not only on the polder I happened to have crossed. *Becoming a_human. A_* standing for *other than* (*autre* in french). Decentralising needs for speciesism.

Hybridization *is* the human impact on the environment by an exhaustive and exploitative so called *culturing* of grounds, lands, arrangement of riverbeds and many beings who cannot be decolonized anymore. May we seek *now for non_intrusive_practices* for we have to take into account that we have (been) altered and cannot recover.

By walking through industrialised territories and by being exposed to smells disturbing my whole senses I felt my body as object of transit. I was in motion, mutating in this environment and could not escape a sourrounding which physically challenged my entire being. Am I *possessing* myself when I shiver? What degree of exposure leads to distress?

Michelle Murphy documents and archives our tendency to become genetically modified at a subtle degree by chemicals that are encoded in our DNA. Where do we go with that? How do we move from t/here? How to imagine becomings? Is our ability to shiver reinforced? How to reformulate motion and language from these points of views that are distorting percievings of our surroundings? We are deeply affected by our close and larger environment. When do we become dependent on substances we are not even aware to accumulate in ourselves? What/when is the tipping point? To what extend do backlashes affect us? What norm states the *normal*? Are we blurring boundaries? How is this bound to our existence/s? Low or below? How low is low? Can we envision presences which we did not choose do assimiliate? Some of us might be in constant struggle to feel/of feeling, exhausted by this *other*. Our territories are soaked by chemicals (refering here to Johanna Hedva's writings and life). How intense is intensity NOW?[4] Silvia Federici takes a poetic turn, stating that if we consider our *bodies as territrories* or *body alike territories*[5], we can shift our needs and actions from t/here towards more care. She intends to reframe our burdens. We are part of territories, we exist among other presences. May we equally take care of each other. May we co-exist and *prolong our beings in one another* as we expand ourselves *as* territories.

> You then completley change your relathionship to what is inside and outside.

How do we cross and walk (in) these realms? I would like to develop the performativity toxic environments imply.

[3] Murphy, M. (2017). Alterlife and decolonial chemical relations. *Cultural Anthropology, 32*(4)

[4] Johanna Hedva wrote about bodies on strike, about sickness, ability, and analyzes the meaning of these words in her artistic practice. She has a chronic disease and is unable to do what most of us can achieve in everyday life. What happens when bodies have to stay in bed because they cannot reach public spaces to denounce their conditions, what if they suffer because of their pathologized condition and have to rely on social media to voice up? How to speak if you cannot be heard?

See: johannahedva.com; johannahedva.com/SickWoman Theory_Hedva_2020.pdf

[5] Federici, S. (2020). *Par-delà les frontières du corps* [*Beyond the borders of the body*]. Quimperlé: Divergences

I also want to consider alienation through work, reinforced exposure to a dispositive altering the awareness of oneself as skattering. How do these workers endlessly rotating on maintenance sites get affected?

"The machine is not an *it* to be animated, worshipped, and dominated. The machine is us, our processes, an aspect of our embodiment. We can be responsible for machines; *they* do not dominate or threaten us. We are responsible for boundaries; we are they."[6]

[6] Gane, N., & Haraway, D. (2006). When we have never been human, what is to be done? Interview with Donna Haraway. *Theory, Culture & Society, 23*, 145. URL: https://journals.sagepub.com/doi/pdf/10.1177/0263276406069228

"We kind of put a soul into a machine _people gave names to the machines they were working with_

We, collective, speaking for generations, refer to past and future, speak for a use. By using the untapped energy potential of sound, and as example can be taken certain frequencies being able to shatter glass.

Part of techno is literally hearing the machine build into the daily movement of Black bodies, the mimesis of movement morphing later into a technology of rhythm.

The space between the notes and not the notes.

Technique rolls over to the machinic, the automated, the driven, the direct drive, the unrelenting.

Syncopation.

Suspension of the resolution between contradictory but twinned positions. The industrial sound that makes (Detroit) Motor City is a prime source of sonic mimesis.

the missing never recover nor get back

The dropout is essentially a pulling away, an acknowledgement of a presence, an energy that has been removed from itself.

Displacement as universal human experience."[7]

[7] Frieze, J. (2019). *Black to Techno*. An exploration of the radical techno movement that originated in Detroit. URL: https://frieze.com/media/jenn-nkiru-black-techno

Black To Techno by Jenn Nkiru retraces and situates the emergence of Techno due to the industrial production in Detroit. J. N. not only uses documents but also integrates narrations of people as well as film alike scenes rendering a broader understanding. We are brought to an acknowledgement which not only stresses the symptoms which have led to this type of music but also to the recognition that there is hope in any form of altered bodies to create. It might surpass their immediate consciousness. Jenn reflects on the need of human beings/workers to seek for interaction and by having engines for coworkers they tend to start unvolontary mimesis which, when fully assimilated will be comparable to being as machine. Techne, Technique, Techno

"I'm interested in tropes as places where you trip. Tropes are way more than metaphors and metonymies and the narrow orthodox list. Noise is only one figure, one trope that I'm interested in. Tropes are about stuttering's, tripping's. They are about breakdowns and that's why they are creative. That is why you get somewhere you weren't before, because something didn't work."[8]

[8] Gane & Haraway, 2011, p. 147

"Nicholas Gane: In thinking of power in terms of connections, it would seem that it becomes increasingly effective by concentrating 'on boundary conditions and interfaces, on rates of flow across boundaries, not on the integrity of natural objects' (Haraway, 1991). This means, in turn, that resistance – if we can call it that – might play out through the breakdown of communication, or in the formulation of codes that prevent the easy translation of all cultural-natural forms. In light of this, is noise."[9]

[9] ibid., p. 151

I'm interested in the way boundaries can be blurred, tormented, be exhausted and reformulated via gestures, actions, walks throughout these territories which usually do not get along well with indeterminacy, errors and improvisation. It may turn the reference into a reverence as creation by alienated bodies rehearsing life as work, then shifting it to a reclaim for freedom.

With these quotes, I had to give a brief introduction to the movement generated throughout history by these industrialized workplaces because it no longer only relies on the bodies and their sensibility to a specfic environment but on how they adapt and relate to the infrastructure, automation, optimization of time, the speed of machines requiring a generalized fastness, which in turn is intrinsically linked to the ability to get a loan. How can motion even be described there if not as mimesis? Therefore, it seems important to me to enlarge the experience of workplaces with the *grounding* of techno music movements because those are deeply linked to the origins of industrial production sites. Several temporalities overlapp. The bodies working, walking there for maintenance, their movements are tremendously calculated and are precisely executed, and then, on the other hand, the bodies invading empty warehouses invoking haunted motion under shivering frequencies. It becomes a trance, a ritualistic celebration for the ones who had left, who had disappeared among/as the machines. Bodies were and are still so deeply entangled in transfers of energies which they can barely handle. *By walking on this polder I had met them, again.* You will not meet the machine behind the fences and walls at first but then, if you focus on the chaos of sounds occuring all over, it becomes clear that the white noise is an association, accumulation of precise movements of animated beings – may they be human or non-human. The movements a machine requires is an intentional but untold re-calibrating of its co-worker for cooperation. *Therefore, I left the ground of walks for the built entities crawling on it.* Would I become machine? I watched over the fence, I had been in between, I had the luxury to keep the distance. I remember these bodies linked, cursed to one another.

Merging these previous thoughts with Michelle Murphy's observations:

Are altered/ill/poisoned bodies more powerfull? *Empowered* by their physical distorsion? Willing or *able* to produce another kind of movement and art? Do interferences in natural environments have this irredeemable consequence? Could we extend the idea to the fact that the algorithmo-centric-neo-capitalist system in which we are evolving is addressed to *abled-bodi*es? And – regarding our increasingly sickening nature triggered by unethical workplaces and attitudes, substances, which integrated our habitus – might we be perturbing particles no longer fitting in the pattern of the economically sustainable from now on? Or is it that alrgorithmo_ speaking this course/curse is already fully integrated in global procedures?

How can walking be a meeting point as practice of/for economical displacement? Out of reach, as well as reaching out to other possibles.

> From automatism to auto-mutism, which I intend to explain in two ways. 1) as mutant, having mutated or being in process of mutating; 2) as mute.

I imagine that this phrasing introduces a censorship of a new kind. An intertwined connection of procedures altering the very nature and behaviour of a subject as well as having determining consequences relative to identity, voice, speculation, and on the degradation and mutilation of commons.

What do you remember of your own being? When you touch, are touched, is it mutual sensing? Did you connect further? Then you might say, you are one and then were many. How does toxicity affect you?

When you walk, you reach out with your senses, or is it the other way around, that the world reaches out to you via your ability to sense? Is motion, any movement, a way to process this world as worlds in simultanious layers of experiences? What surrounds you now/next? What is pleasure in listening/in sensing? How do you transfer emotional states to *others*? What delay do you sometimes handle when someone/a being evolves in a different temporality? Do you seek for understanding or, more likely, deal with intensity?

Jaime Del Val highlights that "we unfold by moving spaces".[10] We create multiple potential realities by tiny variations. Refering to the quote, it is not necessarily about sound in its broadest sense/meaning but about the potentialties and residues capable of pruducing sound, noise, interferences, turbulences.

Imagine the movements, the walks you did in industrial realms. Could these open a soundscape on their own? If you go as fast as your surrounding goes, if you slow down, speed up, how do you expand and retract multiple timeframes and realities? From which point of view do you watch, do you sense? Can you merge both and keep an omnipotent insight on what happends to your demultiplying perceptions? Can you open yourself to such an exercise and exist as worldly, being impregnated by a free will and absorbing the impulses of the surrounding?

The performativity toxic environments imply relies on the attempt to reframe our connectivity and dissociation with the environment. If we start to turn it the other way around in order to hack oppressive measures, we could avoid to get pathologies assigned.[11]

> Mourning alive bodies.

Urging the encounter with cripple existencies of various *forms*, abled-bodies are temporarily unabled; chronic suffering and pathologized destinies propose layers of imagining, different presents and presences. Rethinking our functionnality not as an ultimate goal to reach but to unlock patterns and structures which are invasive. Intending to celebrate, reclaim and rescape motion as a flow and as perception. And in this sense, reformulating languages, spaces and realities. Maybe it is not

---

10 About Jaime Del Val's work: metabody.eu/imf-2021/

11 The Air Syndrome is another example of the so pretended unexplain-able, luckily ephemeral diseases. The symptoms such as nausea and vertigo occure in optimized business buidings. Disfiguring our relationship to our otherworldly extremities and disappear as soon as individuals leave their workplaces (which suddenly seem unappropriate for such purpose). It becomes a time and space related experience: www.epa.gov/sites/production/files/2014-08/documents/sick_building_factsheet.pdf

only about motion but about how movement triggers imaginaries, the so-called spaces which do not exist if not lived.[12]

My relation to walking intends to raise insights in collective memories of lived gestures, may it be as simple as penetrating worlds. I begin to perform and charge improvisations with the need to move backwards. To meet an opening landscape, by not entering it but letting it flow aside. Crawling quite close to the ground, I have the feeling to be way more attentive to what surrounds me by having to rely on other senses than sight to move around in this way. I am more grounded, leaving, weaving movements of care.

[12] About Jaime Del Val's project Metatopia: metabody.eu/metatopia/

The polder I had lived.

The polder I had become.

As extension of frenetic motion. Under the heat I slowed down.
I swallowed.

Animated beings vanishing.

Phoenixes of becomings.

I had worn the yellow transparency, letting me fade,
me, as we, merging into landscapes.

I am about to imagine.

Thresholds we have been walking.

Tracking bodies in transit, shifting archeologies of futures.

Photographs by Maël Cosotti, Brest, workshop with Elvia Teotski, 2021

Hana Magdoňová
39 Days in the Plain

SETTING OFF

I close the tent, checking, if I have all the things I need, put on my backpack and with a bigger or smaller determination, I take my first steps into another day. Through the long grass, I have already trampled a path and I arrive at the asphalt road. By my right side, a few family houses, by my left, a dark forest, at the foot of the Hády hill. After about 200 meters, I turn left on the main road; I am going slightly uphill. From time to time, I have to move to the side because of passing cars. Although the hill is not that steep yet, at this place, I take a little stop every day and for a short moment, I enjoy a view of Brno. Once a day, sunlit; when I return, it is usually already in the dark radiating with a thousand lights. From here, I always send a telepathic greeting to my boyfriend, who is living his life somewhere down there near Špilberk. Well, time to return to my mission! On the right, I see a little path and step on it. And from here on, it really starts! I counted three hundred steps up a steep hill. Passing green grass, flowers in the bloom, and steppe bushes growing no higher than to my knees, I slowly climb up, already knowing my pace to be able to keep my breath so I don't have to stop till the very top. The path is curving and rising, the bushes grow taller and taller and finally, very unexpectedly, the new horizon opens up and my breath is gone at last. Here I am, here I belong, and here I transform.

THE BIRTH OF THE ENVIRONMENT

The very name of the place – Hádecký Kopec (Hády hill) is originally based on the German word Heide which means heath. Nevertheless, the then-existing hill must have had a completely different appearance than today. The place, which was historically reserved for pastures, radically transformed in the 1960s with the start of limestone mining; the hill gradually turned into a surface quarry. In the first phase, two flat quarry walls were created on two sides of the hill – Džungle and Růženin lom. As the mining in these areas was terminated first, the re-cultivation is already in an advanced state. Today, Džungle (the jungle) is a family excursion destination with a Lama Center, managed by the Hády Land Association, which also takes care of the overall maintenance and recultivation of the former quarry. The former mining grounds are now a protected landscape area. Růženin lom (Rosie's quarry), on the other hand, thanks to its charming geodesy, budding flora, and lakes, attracts a completely different group of visitors. Within this magical space, a nudist bathing culture creates an energy full of sexuality, as if you were to appear suddenly in the space of Shakespeare's Midsummer Night's Dream. In the second phase, between these flat quarry walls, mining continued until 1997, the so-called storey type, so a stepped terrace was created here. This layered landscape overlooks Brno with its typical face and is visible from afar. Potassium, which appeared here after the mining, has created a unique flora; for this reason, many of the former quarries have become arboretums during the phase of recultivation.

ENTERING THE PLAIN

Through the whole northside horizon extends a mountain. Mmm... not really a mountain, more like a four-stepped wall. They called it a surface panoramic storey quarry. And here, at the very bottom in the very last story, the deepest mining point, I have found my kingdom: A plain full of nothing, resting in peace surrounded by higher terrain; just the west side extends into the sky. And exactly from here, I enter passing a board which informs about unique animals living in this quarry and currently also about my stay. I am passing the connecting path from lower to the upper storey which creates an imaginary border to my plain. Here, I stay... So what exactly am I doing here, in a book about walking?

THE CONCEPT

When I appeared in Brno about three years ago as a fresh student of the studio of Performance Art at the Faculty of Fine Arts in Brno, I was attracted by a dominant transmitter perched on an inhospitable stone hill without greenery on the horizon during my walks through the new city. I remember my first visit when, during a long hot summer day. I set out from the nearby Líšeň housing estate and looked for paths to the heart of this space which had always been just a horizon for me. After a challenging ascent, I found myself a little breathless in the basin of the lowest floor of the lunar landscape, so much in contrast to the steppe greenery just a few meters below. Surrounded by a stony and raw emptiness, I felt swallowed by this immersive atmosphere. I felt the effect of this landscape on the mood of my inner landscape. Just being there meant to enjoy the experience of something else, something very distant from the normal course of the world and everyday reality. In this area, I did not notice any signs of a close civilization in Brno that would remind me of my place in society. At the same time, however, I could not even succumb to the romantic sentimentality that usually overtakes me in direct confrontation with unspoiled nature full of greenery and biological diversity. I simply found myself in an unfamiliar environment to which I could not have a proper relationship based on experience or an emotionally charged memory. The landscape was empty and free to be exactly what it was, and so I could be as well undiscovered, inexperienced, undescribed... I think that the association with the Biblical story of Jesus' 40-day stay in the desert and the opportunity to experience a similar almost mythological experience came to me exactly during that first visit. And so the project "39 days" emerged.

THROUGH THE PLAIN

I do not know how many steps, or meters it takes to cross the whole plain. I would say about a four-minute walk – but it really depends on my pace. So let's go! Which way of walking will I choose today to cross? You can close your eyes and simply follow your steps; this is the easiest way to figure out that the plain is not plain at all! The first part goes a little bit up and after half the way, it suddenly descends more than it looks like! With your closed eyes, you can find a quicker and less strenuous walk. Your steps are getting lighter as you continue walking. Or perhaps we can take a walk-through one more time! Facing your feet, follow every step through the changing surface. Stones, grass, blossoms, dry mud, gravel, moss, bushes are darting under my feet. It is exciting to observe the changes over the course of my stay. Just within a few weeks, the colors of blossoms change significantly. The color of grass gradually greens and pales depending on the weather. But let's hit the road one more time, and perhaps we can notice other points of view. This time, let's walk with our heads held high, gazing up. This time, our walk is much less steady and it is easy to stumble over a stone or bump into a bush. But what an unusual feeling it is! Our gaze is up and stable rocks are suddenly moving and shaking through our unstable walk. And with this, we finally arrive at the very bottom of the plain at my 'sacrifice stone'. Here, I usually start my mornings with a meditation and my favorite west view into the falling sky on the horizon.

MOTIVATION

The essential experience from the first visit and its gradual rational processing led me to the concept of a 39-day stay. I wanted to prolong the immersive experience I had had during those few hours of my visit – and gradually faded – and monitor its effect on my perception, on changes in my mind and body. As I began to think more specifically about it, I began to perceive the possible (theoretical?) value that my residence could have. From a certain point of view, this event could be described as a kind of anthropological research of one's inner self, a need for a contemporary person to go through the experience of a transition ritual. Within Performance Studies, there would perhaps not be much doubt about the performative effect of doing this stay. But would this act also have value in Performance Art, when the presence of the spectator as a witness is missing? *It is said that beauty is in the eyes of the observer, but what if no one is looking anymore?*[1]

[1] From Leos CARAX' movie Holy Motors, 2012

CRISS CROSS

After meditation, I open my eyes. What will happen next? I have the whole day to spend here. Actually, I have 39 days to spend without any previous plan. I just threw myself here, into this limited space – and what feels like an unlimited time. So I just wait for a moment to see what is necessary or important for me to do now. Perhaps I can visit my music stone on the northeast side of the quarry. I jump on my feet and start to play my flute against the wind. Just a few dozen steps from here is the only tree which provides enough shadow in the days when the sun is uncompromising. I can fit here in a lying position that allows me to read or pursue doing nothing. Not far from here stands the wooden totem in a stone circle – the only thing I built here. With a bent back, I picked stones to build a solid circle and later on created a sun clock from the totem. And just a few steps from here, in the center direction of the plain, rests a little wooden bollard. I have never figured out why it is there... Perhaps simply just for me because it is my favorite place. I meditate here at least a few times a day and with the first opening of my eyes, I see the spectacular walls of the quarry. And from here, just a few meters south, one finds a unique seasonal mini-pond. It is the most changing environment in the plain I can observe. When it rains, a little

pond appears, stays for a few days, and later turns into mud which dries more and more till the soil starts to crack reminding me of old skin or tree bark. It is fascinating to observe those changes. This pond is close to the little path which crosses my plain. I take this path every time I need to go to the toilet to disappear from the scene for a moment... I wish I could see my crisscrossing between my most favorite places from the bird's eye perspective. My patterns of walking would look like patterns of ants, which seem very confusing from my perspective just because I don't know the purpose of the movement.

SUDDEN IMPULSE

After a long stretch of sitting by the wooden bollard, I suddenly stand up and stretch myself... Blackness in front of my eyes; for a while, my whole body is in a state of unknown surprise. Vacuum around me. Now! That's it! Something is happening in my head! This is really something! That is a very different state of being from my normal one! The world is upside down. Is it just in my head or does it affect the whole body? Do I just feel it or is it somehow recognizable also from outside? Now! Let's use this different moment! It is necessary to act now! I have no plan, I just listen to my body. I run away and surrender to the unknown. I cannot see things further than half a step in front of me. No further than to the tip of my toe. This impulse is running with me back and forth. It changes my steps by itself: Once they are tiny, then it is stepping, then it creates long-striding moves. Wow! I just follow my random movement through the plain. My instant being-in-movement naturally protects me from falling. Here, I crash into the bush, there, I jump on the lower stone just like that! And I just go on and on. I feel so funny! Such childish, nonsense behavior! Why can't that happen a few times a day? What could stop me? I don't recognize any borders! Because I feel like I could run like that endlessly... And yet, something comes from inside of my head. Well, Hana, that should be enough! How long do you think you can run like that? You know, you have to stop somehow soon, how will you do it? And I guess, in the end, I really did... Obviously, the only border is my own head. But I wonder: What is the source of the impulse which created such an unreal and unexpected movement? How does my body know it is ready for this kind of experience?

WALK OF STONE

Over and over again, I am witnessing how the elements are shaping the plain. The sun is burning, bursting the soil and cracking the stone. The wind can be sharp here, it crashes into the rocks and gets into the smallest clefts in the minerals. And then, there is rain which is usually very helpful and brings this needed freshness with it. But I saw a downpour with millions of drops hitting the ground that was louder than the thunder. The bare rock transformed into a river with wild little waterfalls. As we usually perceive stone as stable and unchanging, this experience gave me an experience that stone is subject to quick changes as well. With human interventions, the surface was uncovered and the mass of stone developing and forming for millions of years is bare and uncovered like flesh in an open wound. The environment was scarred in a way that cannot be fixed. What humans started, nature continues and in the very slow process of weather effects the stone crumbles into dust. The tiny rock sprinkles somehow remind me of falling tears in the scarred face. Although it is just a rock, I cannot defend myself from sadness. After all, the principle is the same as killing or mutilating a human or animal. Being in a transformative process here myself, I feel strangely humbled facing processes that involve traces from thousands of years.

PRACTICE

As part of the daily practice of my 39-day residency, I focused mainly on the lived experience. By simply being and especially by being aware of my being, I was able to notice and record changes over time in my mind and my body. It is this gradual transformation of the human being that I perceive as artistically valuable in this project. It is a work that is created through the lived space-time experience – it is influenced as well as it influences itself. In this way, artists do not have a subjective power to create their own world but rather experience becoming part of a broader interspecies complex and non-human environment. Various exercises I developed focus mainly on expanding or shifting sensory perceptions; simple work with my body and spirit has also become an important part of everyday practice. I drew inspiration both from various spiritual practices (like Vedic Yoga practice, working with the practices of the Q'ero Natives from Peru, and contemporary witch practice in line with Carlos Castaneda) and from various artistic and performative practices (Miloš Šejn, Tomáš Ruller, Petr Váša, Roberta Legros Štěpánková, Lea Maria Spahn) but in the end, it was mainly my own spontaneous reaction to the local environment.

CLEANING TIME

With a hunched back, I am very slowly proceeding step by step, searching attentively every inch of the ground. My eyes slide from the dry grass to gravel, then from the moss to stones, from stones to garbage, the evidence of the human presence here. Even though I decided to not leave any material traces after my residence, here I am, collecting garbage. Humans, you were here indeed! Beer cans, little plastic particles, aluminum from burnt candles, etc. Step by step,

I am combing through the surroundings, trying not to miss a single spot. When I see something, I slowly bend my back and knees, pick up the thing and slowly stand up again to throw it in the trash bag and walk on. The environment is changing slowly under my feet and I can dive into every detail of the terrain. Over time, my eyes are getting trained to see what is necessary, they are sharpened to see the hunted objects. When I see another piece of glass, perhaps a bottle again, I kneel and pick one piece after another. From time to time, I also encounter old bones lying here, whitening in the sun. Those I am taking for myself, they are my shamanic reward. But the most important reward is the walk itself. In this slow Zen-like pace, I experience care, beneficial for both sides. I finish simply when I feel it and wherever I am. I take the walk back to my sacrificial stone to store the trash and put the newfound bones on the stone. Although my trained eyes can notice more garbage on my way back, I am not picking anymore. My meditation has finished.

THEORETICAL FRAMING

According to Erika Fischer-Lichte's Performative Aesthetics[2], the relationship between performer and audience is a key principle for the emergence of a performative event. The so-called *autopoietic feedback loop* constantly receives and integrates unplanned and unpredictable elements that arise from their mutual interaction. However, as these rules apply to art to be able to emerge, they can also be found in patterns outside of human society: Donna Haraway[3] also works with the term feedback loop but in the field of *Posthumanist Theory*. She refers to a mutual *sympoietic* interaction of natural systems which interact with each other without central control, without temporal or spatial boundaries. As part of my artistic research, I would like to perceive the performer and her body in these biological connotations. My interest is to shift the focus from the anthropocentric focus on human relationships to an interspecies scope, relationality, and posthuman experience. In Haraway's words, we could call it a change in interspecies relationships from *Godkin* to *Oddkin*. The feedback loop should therefore refer to the relationship between the performer and the systems present in the quarry environment.

[2] Fischer-Lichte, E. (2008). *Transformative power of performance.* Oxon: Routledge

[3] Haraway, D. J. (2017). *Staying with the trouble.* Durham: Duke University Press

INTERSPECIES MISUNDERSTANDING

I remember picking up one bigger piece of plastic and, to my surprise, discovered an ant colony right beneath it. Suddenly uncovered, they were quickly moving away and pulling their larvae out of the sun deeper into the anthill. I watched the whole scene quite perplexed and after a short time, the scene was empty like it had never happened; I was quite unsettled. Should I just put the plastic back where it was? Or should I rather throw it away as I had already picked it up now? I was so convinced about my positive contribution cleaning the space of garbage but it already had a different purpose within the interspecies relationships I had not seen. Nature-culture processes where life grows on!

WALK EXERCISE

One of my usual time-killers here is developing different body/senses-oriented exercises to constantly tempt my consciousness and therefore slowly change my way of perceiving. Of course, I could find a seductive ultra-intellectual phenomenological theory to frame this. But somehow still very theoretical... Fortunately, I am a performer in the first place, so all of those fancy ideals are primarily intellectual excuses to wildly experiment with different states of consciousness giving my mind a great shock of realization that sense perception might change in such an enormous way! So let's have an example: In a relaxed walk, I simply march through my plain in very accidental directions. I concentrate my focus on my feet, more exactly to the touch which develops from my steps meeting the ground. Somehow it affects me as independent quality or perhaps even entity which is created by two independent subjects. My movement is the active actor and the ground is more like an adequate responder and their meeting is always and again re-presented with awareness of the new touch/step. I can fully focus on the quality of the touch itself as it is. Or I can experiment further! I stay with the experience of how this touch goes through my whole leg. Starts in the feet and continues not just to the hips but even to the waist; it influences the whole lower part of my body. This visualization (or even better: this experienced sensation) extends the length of my legs because I can feel the movement of walking to the height of my waist. And here the fun starts! How does the brain cope with that kind of experience? It just naturally changes the perspective! So I am able to perceive myself a few centimeters higher than before. So here I come, back and forth accidentally through the landscape and simply grow! And that is just a mind-blowing experience for me! Alice in Wonderland, here I come!

METHODOLOGY

As for the methodology itself, how to deepen, sensitize, and research this relationship? Performative Aesthetics already functions in principle as a living experience and doing and thus has the potential for practical application of Posthumanist Theory. I base this statement again on the common concepts and sources of both. In both of them, there is an obvious appeal to the human bodily transfiguration, which is necessary both for performative action as well as overcoming an anachronic humanist view of the world. Fischer-Lichte, like posthumanist theorist Astrida Neimanis[4], refers at this point to the concept of Maurice Merleau-Ponty[5] who argues that bodily existence is a return to things themselves, that the body is not something we have (having a body), but it is something we inevitably are (being a body). We only have the world because we live as bodies that know the world as an extension of the ways in which the body is. The ability to realize the biological nature of our bodies through *embodiment* expands our experience of the world and our potential for the transformation needed for human sustainability on the planet. The body does not know the state of being, it knows being only in the form of constant change and the process of *becoming*. With each blink, breath, and movement, it re-forms, becomes different, re-embodies.

[4] Neimanis, A. (2017). *Bodies of water.* London: Bloomsbury Academic

[5] Merleau-Ponty, M. (1962). *Phenomenology of perception.* New York: Routledge

THE PATH OF THE COURSE

The environment is slowly taking over control. For a while, I tried to escape from here unconsciously, just to survive the suffering and get out of here. Now, I am trying to squish every minute of my presence. I've got used to the wind which touches every single leaf of each tree and embraces the sound and movement into one continuity which horizontally flows through me – like the swell of the ocean. You can feel it, you can notice it somewhere behind your left ear, but you cannot turn back to see it. All my senses are in a kind of liminal state of being. They accept but do not define. My perception of reality is not contained just in my own body and thoughts anymore. All this surrounding environment is my integral part. I perceive myself as a body in context, an element in the environmental picture. My period let me know about its arrival and my half-awake mind in a sensitive fragile body shell stays kind of numb the whole day long. My weakness is more about becoming than being. I am losing my rational and physical dominance and (finally!) I am letting processes happen freely in their own will, including mine. My walk is kind of purposeless. I am looking around the whole environment or into specific detail, but there are no thoughts or emotions. It is more like the curiosity of children. You can see something, but do not name it. I perceive objects, and then they blur out of focus and merge with their surroundings. Let them work in your unconscious reality and this (non)form marks itself to your memory trace. And this is how I rediscover the lost time of my childhood experiences and abilities which can be very helpful to create a gradual re-formation of perception of learned patterns of reality.

COSMIC WALK

Day by day, I am witnessing the course of the sun in its orbit. The quarry wall is more centered southwest, so I miss the sunrise and morning sun walk. But somehow, I appreciate the peaceful beginning and calm midday time before the sun transforms my plain into a desert-like hearth, especially in the second part of the project. From now on, it is almost impossible to recognize the movement of the planets. For a few hours it seems the sun is almost stuck in one place in the sky. And during those last days, it minimizes my movement as well. Covered by the shadows of the bush I have to lay down because it is too low to be able to sit here. I am melting into not-doing. I am listening to the movement of wind in the leaves, passing tree by tree. I am observing the emerging, existing, and vanishing white lines from airplanes and I am wondering: Will the airplane disappear behind the horizon, or does it just become smaller and smaller till it finally vanishes in the space of blue eternity? What's the time? Or perhaps, what does it matter? It is very hard to think about linear movement in this kind of existence... But somehow it finally happens, like every other day and the sun approaches the west. Wow! Now the time has finally accelerated! I cannot believe that the sun travels at this quick speed the whole day long! And suddenly everything quiets! Everything and everyone in the quarry focuses their attention on the direction of the uncompromising sun, we are all together experiencing the interplanetary movement and kind of common sadness and anxiety passing through this moment. *La petite mort.* What did I do with my time today? Did I spend it well? Could be better... Perhaps tomorrow then? It is just a short moment of facing the west. Everything dies to rise with the new day again. From the sunset on to sunrise and then again, another day will start as usual.

Otto Kauppinen
Walking and Physical Movement as a Vehicle of Immersion

Participation in Czech performative projects at Prague Quadrennial 2019

INTRODUCTION

Writing this text at the end of 2021, the performative art scene in Middle Europe has been, with some breaks, mostly shut down since 2020, and the emergence of new influential pieces has been minimal. Having the time to look back, I decided to revisit Prague Quadrennial (PQ) 2019 and to look at two interesting projects introduced there through the perspective of walking and physical movement. With that said, even this article has been *affected by the coronavirus pandemic,* because due to a lockdown in Slovakia at the end of November 2021 I could not see a new project that is in a sense a continuation of one of the projects I will be writing about. Nonetheless, the situation is how it is and we can only hope performative art will be able to *walk* out of it sometime soon.

If we think about going to the theatre, most of us imagine *sitting* being a position they would expect to perceive a theatre piece in. Even if not restricting a spectator to being a passive "actor" in the autopoietic feedback loop, as Erika Fischer-Lichte[1] argues, and granting a spectator a position to *"observe, choose, compare, interpret"*[2], as Jacques Rancière states, sitting is still a position inviting a physically passive role in the relational web of the theatre space. To physically interact with something outside of your nearest vicinity, you would need to stand up first.

[1] Fischer-Lichte, E. (2011). *Estetika performativity* [*The aesthetics of performativity*]. Mníšek pod Brdy: Na konári, p. 55

[2] Rancière, J. (2015). *Emancipovaný divák* [*The emancipated spectator*]. Bratislava: Divadelný ústav, pp. 16–17

The element of choice between different stages or actions that the performance consists of is often called "immersive theatre". It is a theatre piece or performance that is happening in a larger environment where spectators are able to move freely and experience the different 'stages' at their own pace, in their own order. The non-restricted movement is a very strong aspect of a piece. It seemingly frees spectators from a fixed perspective where the 'theatre illusion' is needed to make them involved in the worldbuilding and allows them to be an embodied part of that world moving through it similarly to performers and thus being 'immersed' into it. Let´s look at an example of this approach from PQ 2019.

CAMPQ

The official Czech presentation of scenography at Prague Quadrennial of Performance Design and Space in 2019 was a multi-layered project called CAMPQ. Spatially, it was divided between a pavilion at the main festival venue on the Prague Exhibition Ground in Prague-Holešovice and a large space at the Štvanice island in central Prague. The pavilion at the festival venue was basically only an advertisement for the real Czech exhibition on the island. The whole project was covered by a fictitious narrative: several distinct alien species arrived on Earth to seek asylum there. An integration camp for alien beings was established by the Government Agency for Integrating Alien Civilizations. In this narrative, the pavilion at the Exhibition Center served as a reception, where festival guests could sign up for a bus trip to the island and buy a ticket for the performance. Half of the island was transformed into a stage for an immersive theatre performance also called *CAMPQ* which was a humongous project involving four directors, four playwrights, almost a dozen stage designers, and approximately sixty performers. The stage design for the performance was actually the Czech exhibition for PQ 2019, and the performance explored the story around it. Shortly after seeing the piece, I wrote a review on it which was published in the Czech Theatre Newspaper (Divadelní noviny), so I will skip further introduction here as it is available in that article.[3] Let´s see how the aspect of physical movement in this immersive piece influenced my view of the artwork.

The fictitious integration camp consisted of many structures that served their function in the narrative: from human infrastructures like medical facility and camp defense HQ through theatre stage, snack and beer stands (that served their real function also) to the living quarters of the aliens – containers and a hive of the alien queen. From a purely visual perspective, these structures were nothing spectacular until the night came and the dreamy, atmospheric lighting connected the whole island to the living city (and to a degree helped with suspension of disbelief). The performance itself, after an energetic beginning, had a quite loose structure where spectators could move from one stage to another by their free will. Unfortunately, non-Czech-speakers were robbed of this freedom as (shockingly for a project prepared for an international festival with a text written by both Czech and Catalonian authors) the whole piece was only in Czech and they needed to follow interpreters. The loose pacing had paradoxically an activating effect on me: Rather than being indecisive about what to do, I tried to explore the area and find clues about possible side motives of the alien presence that were hinted at before. The actors reacted to my questions quite spontaneously and managed to keep the artistic stylization of their particular species: The cyborg-like "Zeyris" continued to move their lips even when not talking which created a feeling that they are always taking part in numerous conversations via their clearly visible hi-tech implants, the fast neurotic movement of ant-like "Attas" as they took care of their queen created a truly non-human vibe, and stoic calmness of the enigmatic "Phoenix women" waiting for their inevitable death and resurrection as a natural part of their life-cycle managed to be fascinating and unnerving at the same time.

There was also a higher level of participation involving movement for randomly selected spectators, luckily me being one of them. Some spectators were 'recruited' to play 'anti-alien activists', some to play 'camp defense force' later on (that was my case). After 'activation' of us 'sleeper agents', we went through a short 'training course' involving running circles and doing push-ups to test our stamina. Even if the actors were not convincing as strict drill sergeants, the physical exertion instantly pumped my immersion up. Suddenly, feeling the rough ground of the main camp road and the softness of the hill where the alien homes were built by running there added something to my experience that was not there before. Being able to exhaust my body even a little bit made me feel like being part of the fictional situation where the riot in the camp was being violently suppressed, as its fictional inhabitants were also under stress and physically tired. This is where the piece was closest to the meaning of the term "immersive" for me: being an actor[4] in a situation where my body is experiencing the same physical movement as the body of a performer. Usually, in (physical) theatre, we can only experience the physicality of the performer by comparing our previous experience of similar movement with what we are seeing, as Finnish researcher Saara Moisio argues.[5] For this moment, *CAMPQ* managed to immerse me by allowing me to become part

[3] Kauppinen, O. (2019). CAMPQ. Chci uvěřit... [*CAMPQ. I want to believe...*]. *Divadelní noviny, 28*(13), p. 4. Prague: Společnost pro Divadelní noviny. URL: https://www.divadelni-noviny.cz/campq-chci-uverit

[4] By "actor" I mean the term used by Fischer-Lichte to define the active participant of the feedback loop who, by physically participating, makes the spectators react and thus create a co-play between them, enabling theatre to emerge. Fischer-Lichte, 2011, p. 51

[5] Moisio, S. (2021). *Ei nykytanssia tarvitse ymmärtää – vai tarvitseeko?* [*You don't need to understand contemporary dance – or do you?*]. *Teatteri & Tanssi+Sirkus, 10*(2–3). Helsinki: Kustannusosakeyhtiö Teatteri, 34–37

of the story and playing a part in it. But this experience also swiftly revealed the shortcoming of the frame in which we were supposed to move. After being ordered to guard a location and prevent other spectators to enter, I got quite involved and started to arbitrarily act on my own and improve our 'strategy'. But actors playing my superiors ignored me or even tried to stop me from doing anything else than they were doing. They were clearly not prepared for such an active intervention and were just acting within the borders of the artistic concept. As Claire Bishop argues, this kind of participation, even when it is physical, is not freeing the spectator but rather submitting him to the will of the artist.[6]

[6] Bishop, C. (2012). *Artificial hells: Participatory art and the politics of spectatorship.* London: Verso, p. 277

PRAGUE IS NOT CZECH

At PQ 2019 there was another case of using common traveling and movement as means of creating a shared immersive experience. The project was called *Prague is not Czech* (Praha není Česko) and it was developed by students of stage design at Janáček Academy of Performing Arts in Brno.

On the first look, the concept had some similarities to CAMPQ. The exhibition at the festival venue consisted of a newspaper stand instantly recognizable by every Czech as a traditional newsstand from the socialist era. But the newsstand itself was only the external part of the whole concept. There was a big sign "Prague is not Czech" on the stand which stood for a travel agency run by the Intellectrurally Collective (kolektiv Intelektrurálně) as the students had named themselves. The collective[7] is a holder of the Imagination Award in Student Exhibition from Prague Quadrennial 2019. In their manifesto they wrote:

[7] The collective consists of scenographer and curator Anna Chrtková who studied Scenography at Theatre Faculty of Janáček Academy of Music and Performing Arts in Brno and Interactive Media Theory at the Faculty of Arts, Masaryk University, Brno; fine artist Andrea Dudková who studied Scenography at JAMU in Brno and who now studies at the Environment Studio in the Faculty of Fine Arts, Brno University of Technology; and visual artist Jan Matýsek who also studied Scenography at JAMU and in the Studio of Painting and Graphic Design at the Faculty of Fine Arts at FAVU. Now he is studying at Academy of Fine Arts in Prague in Studio of New Media II.

> *We are a travel agency and an artistic project at the same time. We search for contemporary Czechness.*
>
> *We are observing while being observed and the notion of "Czechness" helps us to understand what is real, local, and important.*
>
> *We respect what is around us. We do not have a plot, a text, a scenario. We work with the non-expected; we expect meetings with locals, diversity of opinions.*
>
> *We focus on places that simply exist. Places where there is nothing, where nothing awaits, and where no one expects us. In such places, we have to make some effort. Find our way of having fun, find the willingness to start a dialogue. We are not designers. We refuse to hide ourselves inside the black boxes or white cubes, we do not need to build something that already exists outside of them. We create a situation that lives on its own.*
>
> *Sometimes it is important to fight off the fear of choosing the haircut from the provincial salon catalog.*[8]

[8] Bulandrová, A., Chrtková, A., & Dudková, A. (2021). Prague is not Czech: Artistic project as a public service. *Amfiteater: Journal of Performing Arts Theory, 9*(1), 185–192. URL: https://www.slogi.si/wp-content/uploads/2021/07/Amfiteater_9_1_RAZ_08_The-Intelektruralne-Collective_EN.pdf

These ideas were incorporated into the concept of the travel agency in the form of specific trips that could be bought at the festival booth. Even if the travel agency was created only as a part of the project for the Quadrennial, it transcended its duration and continued offering performative trips even some months after that. That means it cannot be easily labeled as fictitious. In this way, the project created an immersive experience as you booked the trip just like any other trip. The PR and advertisement for *Prague is not Czech* were similar to the vocabulary of commercial travel companies to show how empty this PR language is when confronted with "real Czechness" that the trips showed the participants. The similarities to *CAMPQ* in a sense of having a reception at the Exhibition Ground and the artwork being experienced elsewhere end here; *Prague is not Czech* is not theatre in the traditional sense. It is more of a play with reality and relations between the trip participants. I will expand on this argument later in the text.

The white news booth stood out in the Quadriennal lobby among most of the other pavilions which were much more stylized. It was a village diorama all with a fence, bush, tables, and chairs in front of it where people casually drank coffee and beer that one could buy at the stand while watching something on a TV screen. Some of them were just having their money cleaned by a performer who made 'baths' for the health of our hard-earned currency – another service that could be purchased at the stand.

Being curious about all that, I went to the stand itself. I observed postcards with various Czech regional locations with a "Prague is not Czech" – sticker attached to them in truly DIY style. A smiling young woman with a missing front tooth asked me what type of travel I would be interested in. I thought for a while and said: *"I would like to find out what real Czechness is."* She offered me a catalog with six travels they were offering; each was labeled with a number of stars to indicate how difficult they would be to endure physically and mentally. I smiled as I realized that usually, travel agencies rank the luxury level of travel in this way. Even when all the trips were curated by *Prague is not Czech*, the collective members created and participated only in one of them. All the others were organized by students from different art schools (Faculty of Fine Arts at the Brno University of Technology, Theatre Faculty of Academy of Performing Arts in Prague, Janáček Academy of Music and Performing Arts in Brno) and other artistic groups as independent artworks. In this way, *Prague is not Czech* brought different collectives together while maintaining a clear artistic vision. Most of the trips, which included traditional hiking, mushroom picking, meeting mythological creatures, and a commentary on social or architectural problems, also included a common walk.

"I think you would love the trip called 'No pie to munch on without hard work'" (Bez práce nejsou koláče), recommended the woman. This one being organized by Intelectrurally themselves, I accepted her offer and bought a ticket which came with a train ticket as well. Then, I sat for a while at the table and enjoyed a cup of strong black coffee with grounds.

On the morning of the travel, I was supposed to meet with other trip participants in front of the Prague Main Train Station. Unfortunately, I slept a little too long and was a few minutes late for the meeting. Fortunately, the group was recognizable by a 'stewardess' holding a sign with "Prague is not Czech" written on it (which I recognized as the woman without a front tooth who sold me the ticket) who assured me that we were still waiting for someone. After she received a call that said person is not coming, the whole group, consisting of approx. 15 people from both Czech Republic and other countries, was led by the stewardess to the train which took us out of the city.

The landscape changed from urban to industrial soon, which then disappeared quickly in the midday sun when the train entered the surrounding fields. I suddenly realized that I was hungry, as I missed my breakfast. The stewardess was quick to address this issue by distributing food packages to the participants. Those consisted of Czech white bread (rohlik) and spreads or cheeses, and a small juice pack (Fruko). The last time I had had this humble combination was in my childhood traveling the countryside with my parents. A participant sitting next to me was definitely expecting something else for the snack and looked a little bit confused. He looked even more confused when the stewardess pulled a few beers out of her bag. I felt like encouraging him so I uncorked the beer, took a sip, and, to his excitement, offered it to him.

It turned out that the other participant was a theatre director from China and a very polite and insightful conversation partner. The conversation in the compartment became more relaxed as more participants joined. The poppy fields the train was passing by became another big topic for conversation. Many foreigners could not understand that it is not illegal to grow poppy seeds in Czech. The common snack loosened the atmosphere quite a bit.

When the train arrived near Podůlšany village, the group was greeted by another 'Prague is not Czech'-team member who guided the group into the village. The team member was carrying a camera and that was when I realized the purpose of the TV screen at the newsstand: She was live-streaming the journey to the booth at the Quadrennial. I did not feel uncomfortable in front of the camera; I was rather lost in thoughts about being in the center of Prague hour ago and now being somewhere in the middle of the countryside but still bringing along the 'Pragueness' with the foreigners around me and with my mindset of going on festival activity to analyze art. But I also realized I already started losing it: I really enjoyed the train ride and showed my new Chinese friend some good old Czech habits.

In the nearby village, we were led to a specific house to get rid of our bags, then the whole group continued the trip by walking several kilometers to a large strawberry field behind the village. Introducing the field and showing how to properly pick a strawberry, the owner let us in. The next hour or so was spent squatting in the field, picking strawberries, comparing their funny shapes with other participants, sweating in the sun, getting a little dirty, and doing other stuff that the viewers at the booth at Quadriennal pavilion could only dream of. At last, the baskets were filled and we walked back to the village. The official goal of the trip was to make traditional Czech strawberry dumplings from the picked strawberries. The process of co-operative cooking was led by the enthusiastic Lenka, the owner of the house and a very authentic and spontaneous village woman, who seemed pleased that a group of strangers came to her house to cook with her. *"There is no food without work",* she said commenting on the picked strawberries.

The notion of "making an effort" from the manifesto came to my mind. We are so used to having everything prepared for us at organized trips that having to actually do something is in a sense opening us more towards the other who would be, in another setting, the one to pick the strawberries for us. The humbleness of picking the strawberries ourselves was thematized in the name of the trip. One could argue that it is somewhat degrading the topic of low-income labor when the strawberry picking becomes a 'staged' situation, a performance even, with participants being able to refuse. But that was not the point of this particular trip while some of the others were focused on that, for example, "Aussig hat Saft und Pizzazz" which toured the participants in marginalized parts of Ústí nad Labem town or "The Real Estates of Spořilov" which explored the original social intention for Spořilov housing estate in Prague. The overall topic of a cultural and social gap between big cities and the periphery was still present even in the journey I experienced:

> "Picking strawberries – which was the objective of one of the trips organized by the Prague is not Czech travel agency – could thus be understood also in terms of 'scenery as a lived space'. (...) The authors of the Prague is not Czech project strived to reflect on the separation of the small local centers, villages and their inhabitants from the capital, and the often very deep chasm of opinions between the inhabitants of cities and rural areas."[9]

[9] ibid., p. 193

Not only getting food requires effort, but also the creation of relationships does. And here the cooking functioned as a perfect medium, with Lenka lightening the situation up now and then with tactless and still heartwarming comments judging the cooking skill of specific participants. Everyone was invited to try their luck at all the stages of preparation from washing the strawberries and rolling dough to forming the dumplings. Because the morning snack was humble, by the time the dumplings were ready everyone was hungry. We gathered around the table, some of us volunteering to fill plates for others. But we started eating only after all plates were filled. The rest of the afternoon was spent on Lenka's veranda drinking beer and socializing with other participants. When the time came to return to Prague, the mutual feeling was that the temporary 'home' was at Lenka's, not at the festival venue.

REALITY AND RELATIONS

The *Prague is not Czech* project can be read as relational art[10] rather than an installation or performance art and the reason for this is the concept of a shared walking trip (obviously there was the train travel as well, but that was more just a means to change location; the traditional concept of Czech walking trip even involves a train ride).

Nicolas Bourriaud defines relational aesthetics as "aesthetic theory consisting in judging artworks based on the inter-human relations which they represent, produce or prompt",[11] and he tracks the roots of relational art to the situationist movement in the fifties and sixties. Bourriaud defined the term for the first time as a curator in a catalog for an exhibition called *Traffic* in the CAPC contemporary art museum in Bordeaux in 1996.[12] As a curator he tried to elaborate on his new concept because most of the mentioned artists became known in the context of relational aesthetics for artworks often including common cooking, eating, listening, or some other shared activity that enables all participants to get involved to the same level; still, the reviews state that concept of the exhibition was not clear because it involved also artworks like painting and video art which do not use human relations, and the exhibition did not establish the term, neither a new artform.[13] In 1998, Bourriad published his thoughts in "Relational Aesthetics" (Engl. 2002). Even if the book was criticized for being just a differently worded thinking about socially critical art, it caused a heated discussion in the western aesthetics circles (one of its biggest critics being Jaques Rancière) about the ever-questioned position of spectators or participants in art.

If we now look at the meaning of the term "immersive", it mostly means the process of being so deeply involved in something that we accept it as a reality (for the moment of immersion). As for the first piece I described I do not think the term "immersive theatre" is very functional for this context because I never really accepted the narrative that the aliens are situated in the middle of Prague; the theatricality of the situations was breaking the illusion for me. The only moments I felt immersed were the moments that involved moving my body to a higher degree. That activation of my body was the vehicle of immersion because it was happening in *reality*, not in my perception of the narrative.

Prague is not Czech on the other hand takes, perhaps presents us our reality in a context that is almost impossible to achieve naturally (cooking strawberry dumplings with a Chinese theatre director in a Czech village). This is what the claim *"to work with the non-expected"* from the Intelectrurally manifesto means. As we saw the impossible manifest before our very eyes, our perception of reality entered a hypersensitive state and we were immersed in the situation we were in. The notion of a common movement, specifically walking in the countryside, made us perceive this reality with our bodies. This reality – the Czech villages and regional culture – is something that many of us remember from childhood (many Czechs spent their childhood in regions and moved to big cities later) or know it from common knowledge, but have not 'walked its surface' themselves.

The trip had a strong aspect of embodiment that was experienced by shared practices of walking, preparing food, and eating. The participants started their trip at the concrete jungle of Main Train Station which has this feeling of flat

[10] Bourriaud, N. (2002). *Relational aesthetics*. Paris: Les Presses du Réel, p. 113

[11] ibid., p. 112

[12] The exhibition included artworks from artists like Rirkrit Tiravanija, Jens Haaning, Vanessa Beecroft or Philippe Parreno.

[13] Tsingou, E. (1997). Traffic. *Zingmagazine – A curatorial crossing*, 3(3). New York: Zing LLC

heaviness and unresponsiveness, but also a feeling of stability when you walk on it. The second phase was the travel by train. The feeling of standing on the uncertain ground when the train shakes, the worry to not spill a drink, the unique experience of instability when using the toilet on the train – this all added up to creating a bodily experience of travelling, of changing space, and made us accept the new environment as 'new'. Experiencing the longer walk on village roads and forest paths immediately after that felt very comforting and freeing as we were not being condemned to the closed space of a train. Stepping into the mud at the strawberry field feels different than stepping into the mud in the city center (if there's even any). The mud in the city feels 'dirty' or 'polluted' in the same way as smog or smoke from traffic because it is alien to us – we do not know its origin, it is just 'universal dirt'. The mud at the strawberry field felt suddenly like 'our' or 'familiar' mud in a sense that we knew why it was there – the strawberries need soil to grow, and the soil becomes mud when it gets wet.

The other bodily aspect of the trip was digestion, or eating and drinking, and how this experience influenced our perception of the artwork. We first experienced it on the train when all participants were given the snack. It started almost as an aesthetic experience at first when the stewardess took the snacks in plastic bags out of her bag. It looked like something my mother would bring on a trip in the nineties – all in non-ecological plastic bags, an unhealthy type of bread, cheap cheese spread, and the children's packaged juice with a straw. Even when this stigma of the nineties floats over these humble delicatessen, consuming them felt so refreshing after being bored to death by the contemporary cuisine meant to please 'foodies' which also has the bitter aftertaste of late capitalism. The sip from a shared beer bottle on a 'official' and organized trip also has this smell of subtle rebellion of school day trips where it meant a lot to do something that is not allowed – a feeling that is so successfully rooted out in many adults, judging from the reactions of some participants. The choice of the main dish – strawberry dumplings – was very inclusive as they are vegan (excluding the hot butter on top) but are also in a way very exotic because having sweet food as a main dish is not traditional in many countries. It is a food with a heart, quite literally, as eating the fruit inside and getting colored red by it is something that associates a cheerful family meeting.

The whole trip created a feeling of really arriving somewhere to spend some time there, and the frame of the train ride brought liminality to getting out of the city. In *CAMPQ*, this was not the case as the bus ride from the festival venue to Štvanice island was optional. The possibility to free roam in *CAMPQ* and other immersive theatre pieces feels like moving the 'camera' or perspective of my field of vision, similarly when you visit a gallery and move your head around the objects there. In projects like *Prague is not Czech* and other (relational) art, the notion of (hyper)reality is the key. Even if the situation itself is to some degree initiated by the artists (and thus "hyper"), as a participant, I am on the same level in the situation as anybody else who is present. In CAMPQ all of my movement was predicted. On the *Prague is not Czech* trip, I could have done basically anything (and I am sure I did!) to break out of the concept and add my own contribution to it, for example, by talking to a random person that we met and who was not part of the trip and having him show me around. By this, I also stretched the space where the trip was happening. This is not an evaluation, just an observation; as a participant (or a spectator of reality?), I breathed much more freely here because I felt that I could not do anything 'wrong'.

CLOSING THOUGHTS

Unfortunately, I cannot write about an upcoming project connected to Intelectrurally Collective, originally scheduled for to end of November 2021, because it is unfortunately postponed for the time being due to another lockdown in Slovakia. It is a project of Anna Chrtková in cooperation with Matyáš Grimmich[14] which promises to explore these bodily encounters in reality even further. The project is called *What if We´re All Pleurisma in Each Other* and was created during their residency at the culture space Nová Cvernovka in Bratislava, Slovakia. The duo focuses on creating the "common Us" by organizing a ten-kilometer walking trip from Bratislava's center to the city outskirts, during which they place a focus on introspection and empathy within the group but also towards the world around:

[14] Prague-based performer and student of painting at Academy of Fine Arts.

> "An allegoric journey about how to create a common Us and what ambitions we can actually have in that. A journey towards a map, not according to one. A path to introspection, empathy, yourself, and others. Our walking speed will be defined by our break-ups and getting together anew. Expect unexpected meetings, pinches to face, some inspirations for the road, ten kilometers behind us, Czech-Slovak sisterhood (and brotherhood), and a bath for the brave ones."[15]

[15] Project website: novacvernovka.eu/program/reaktor-what-if-were-all-pleurisma-in-each-other (here translated by author)

The trip would end in the outskirts of Bratislava allowing all participants to take a common bath in natural hot springs located there. After experiencing a workshop of Matyáš Grimmich this summer who explores means of sharing emotions without talking about them, I believe this artistic duo is a great match and I am looking forward to immersing myself in their reality on their next trip.

Them elsewhere on the website referencing some aspects of this journey as "dinner, fatigue, absolution, and baptism" is again bringing me to thinking about what the format of contemporary theatre performance can be. The journey, as described in the previous citation, consists of common walking with some inspiration, events, and activities brought by the artists. Still, the walk remains a walk, the food break a food break, a meeting a meeting, a bath a bath. Something else is needed to establish the almost sacred notion of perceiving these events as 'dinner, fatigue, absolution, and baptism'. The participants need to agree to look at these events in the way the artist is proposing them to do. They need to accept the invitation.

Semih Firincioğlu argues that the most notable aspect of a "performance" in a broader sense is that the perceiver identifies the event as something worth spectating and acknowledges when it starts and ends.[16] This is something that everyone must do willingly; they can as well refuse and the performance is not happening even if the artist would stand on his/her head. I agree with Chrtková and Grimmich that the format of a common trip is a "low-threshold medium" where this agreement is much more up to the participants and their momentary feelings and relations with the group – and they can decide to accept or refuse it without consequences, as opposed to, for example, theatre performance in a theatre space, where the spectators are expected to accept this agreement at the moment they buy the ticket.

[16] Firincioğlu, Semih (2021). Notes on the Performing Arts 02. What is Performance? New York, performideas.com/2021/07/01/02-what-is-performance/

This has a lot to do with the approach to notice the process of relations between human beings in the space while spectating performative art. Be it the "triadic collusion" of Klaus Lazarowicz[17] or the already mentioned "autopoietic feedback loop" of Fischer-Lichte[18], relations are always happening between performers and spectators (in the case of Lazarowicz also including the author). So the line between those who initiate the relation (actors) and those who make first feedback (spectators) is clearly defined.[19] Even if Fischer-Lichte acknowledges also a physically participating spectator who takes over the role of "actor", and so both roles are fluid, there is still the dominant need to distinguish between those who physically act in the space and those who do not (or do not do it visibly enough). It is not as much about performativity, which can have also very subtle manifestations, as about distinctiveness of the physical expression and the ability to stand out in the space and get attention. The artworks that Bourriaud describes in his book often look at relations in space in a way that cancels such a dichotomy. The important thing is not that the interaction happens between an actor who receives the attention and a spectator that grants him this attention but that it happens between human (or even non-human) beings present at the same time in the same space. Perceiving ourselves *in the context of the presence of all the others* is the thing that gets the attention. Does the other participant need, or even want, my attention at the moment? How is my attention perceived, and where is it needed? How does my focus or shift of attention change the situation (of relations)? These questions should be also asked when thinking about co-existence in space. Regarding this approach, "art is a state of encounter".[20] The physical movement or participation is not initiated by an impulse from the artist but is rather natural to a state of being in the space where the artwork is taking place. Relations can emerge even between participants that never achieve the status of "actor". The artwork is the impulse that creates new relations in the space. And that can be done by anybody present. If Fischer-Lichte writes about "emergence of meaning",[21] Bourriaud sees the *emergence of relations* in art. The temporary community that is created on a walking trip by the shared movement is always moving not only to a goal pinpointed on the map but also to the metaphorical goal of exploring common relations. More than twenty years after being even recognized as a distinct art form, I feel that relational art is expanding from the territory of fine arts and performance also into contemporary theatre, bringing togetherness that stems from the non-hierarchic aspect of it. I believe that the best artwork in the world can strongly resonate within me for a few months, maybe years. But an inter-human relation (and maybe also non-human kinship) which the piece causes to emerge can persist for a lifetime – and can lead to forming something new: a co-working, a friendship, a partnership, or even social change.

[17] Lazarowicz, Klaus (2005). Triadická koluze. Souřadnice a kontexty divadla. Antologie současné německé divadelní teorie, Prague: Divadelní ústav, pp. 23–30

[18] Fischer-Lichte, 2011, p. 69

[19] ibid., p. 51

[20] Bourriaud, Nicolas, 2002, p. 18

[21] Fischer-Lichte, 2011, p. 222

140

3rd Part

Walking as Method(ology)

Shira Wachsmann

The Moment Before – War Trauma, Embodiment, and the Re-Membering of Matter (and what matters)

I wrote this text in the wake of the events of the last escalation in Israel / Palestine in May 2021 and the general associated silencing atmosphere in Germany. On May 10th, Israel launched airstrikes on the Gaza Strip following rocket strikes on the South of Israel by Hamas. At least 256 Palestinians, including 66 children, and 8 Israelis, counting two children, were killed as a result of the violence.

The aftermath of these events led me to focus this text on trauma, boundaries, and the creation of shape and identity as an ideological apparatus, and the reconfiguring of matter or what I call, the re-membering through art practice, or more specifically moving image correspondence.[1] Nevertheless, in this text, I am not referring only to the encounter between humans and themselves, but also to the encounter between humans and other entities or to everything that is in motion in this world.[2]

[1] In this context, I will also talk about a different concept of time that I have developed in connection with my artistic practice.

[2] Golding, J. (2020). The courage to matter. In *Data loam (2020): Sometimes hard, usually soft*. Berlin/Boston: de Gruyter, 450–486

THE MOMENT BEFORE – WAR TRAUMA, EMBODIMENT, AND THE RE-MEMBERING OF MATTER (AND WHAT MATTERS) [3]

My research takes as a starting point that trauma is a living entity. Trauma, war trauma, and possibly all trauma can be seen as a particular set of wounds/scars shaped by memory, fear, identity, and politics. A re-positioning of those scars can reveal not only how their intensity operates in the discourse but also sheds light on how the mechanisms of creating knowledge, identity, and meaning are formed.

In my artworks, and in particular in my last moving image correspondence, I work with different entities that I encounter while moving around in a topology of trauma. I explore the unspoken zone where memory, amnesia, and trauma of war are embodied, preserved, and circulated in the Palestinian/Israeli cactus called Sabra which historically demarcate the boundaries of Palestinian villages and remain a living testament in the landscape of a life lived before 1948. The Sabra (or in its botanical name Opuntia Ficus-indica) originates in Mexico and arrived with the Spanish to the middle east in the 16th century. Until today, it is still unclear if this specific cactus is a man-made assembly from 2 other cacti or a self-evolution of the cactus itself, thus, challenging the accepted dichotomy and binary thought of the clear division between culture and nature and the way it has been used to push forward certain agendas.[4] The change of climate from the Mexican to the middle eastern weather allowed the Sabra to spread only with human cultivation or when branches accidentally fell to the ground and take root. This quality makes them perfect as fences or territorial markers, a practice that was used by the Palestinians and did not change after the British Empire occupied Ottoman Palestine during the First World War. The war of 1948 and its aftermath, however, marked a dramatic change in the social and cultural role of the cacti in the landscape. Israel appropriated the cacti as a symbol of its people, which ultimately led to the popularization of the term Sabar (צבר); once the word for cactus, now also referring to an Israeli-born Jew. During the war, the Palestinian villages were destroyed and their residents were exiled marking the first stage of this metamorphosis – from Palestinian territorial markers to a symbol of recognition for Israel.[5]

In 2005, the term Sabra (cactus) morphed itself once again, but this time into a tank, namely the "Sabra M60T", the main battle tank of the Israeli forces.[6] Thus continuing its transformation from border markers and a symbol of defense to an attacker and an occupier.[7] I am looking at the role of the cactus specifically as a body of a fence, a body that contains a cultural narrative, a collective body of memory and trauma, as a worker and a soldier, and as a body that can be killed.

[3] This text is part of my Ph.D. thesis, which I am currently doing at the Royal College of Art in London. All rights on the text, images, and diagrams belong to Shira Wachsmann.

[4] Griffith, M. P. (2004). The origins of an important cactus crop, *Opuntia ficus-indica* (Cactaceae): New molecular evidence. *American Journal of Botany, 91*(11), 1915–1921

[5] Apel, D. (2012). *War culture and the contest of images*. New Brunswick, NJ & London: Rutgers University Press; Benvenisti, M. (2005). *The dream of the white Sabra*. Jerusalem: Keter Books

[6] See: www.military-today.com/tanks/sabra.htm,

[7] Kimmerling, B. (2001). *The invention and decline of Israeliness: State, society, and the military.* Oakland: University of California Press

I first encountered the sabra through walking. In my childhood, walking along the cactus walls in the forest without knowing that they mark a past territory. Playing with, on, and next to traces of past lives, memories and stories. The cactus is a body that carries counter-memory and language. It contains the memory of the place. They were not uprooted, they still inhabit the space, the earth, the village as a living memory.

Recording the sabra in Sh-Murad cemetery

In my work, I perceive the Sabra as an event that unfolds in different directions, taking on different shapes, meaning, and time periods. My research, and the artistic practice that accompanies it, focuses on the role of trauma and how it is played out and embodied in three main protagonists or entities: the cactus, human, and tank that are haunted by an explosion in some way or another. The explosion or trauma creates two halves and a void: before the explosion, after the explosion, (before the trauma and after the trauma), and the attraction/tension between them.

The effect of trauma is the opposite of linear time. The past is projected into the future coming back to create a segment or the present, creating a fluid environment that allows the living trauma to take shape and circulate.

Diagram of time, 2021: B- before the trauma, A- After the trauma.

I am looking at "the moment before" which is a term that emerged from my practice and came into my theory, where time, trauma, and event intra-act in different ways than the linear time events we normally use.Intra-action is a term introduced by Karen Barad, in which the ability to act is not an inherent property of an individual or human being that can be exercised, but a dynamism of forces in which all ‚things' are constantly exchanging, diffracting, influencing and inseparable. Intra-action also recognizes the impossibility of an absolute separation or classically understood boundaries. The ability to act emerges from within the relationship. And that ability is constantly changing and adapting to the processes in which it is involved. "Existence is not an individual affair. Individuals do not preexist their interactions; rather, individuals emerge through and as part of their entangled intra-relating. This is not to say that emergence happens once and for all, as an event or as a process that takes place according to some external measure of space and of time, but rather that time and space, like matter and meaning, come into existence, are iteratively reconfigured through each intra-action, thereby making it impossible to differentiate in any absolute sense between creation and renewal, beginning and returning, continuity and discontinuity, here and there, past and future."[8] I am looking at the moment before the explosion as simultaneously a segment in space and time, and a wave that diffracts and becomes the unfolding event. As we can see in this diagram of time I made, time is much more dimensional than linear and the present depends on the way we will remember the past and re-member the future. The past and future are always active in the present, they are entangled and inseparable.

[8] Barad, K. (2007). *Meeting the universe halfway: Quantum physics and the entanglement of matter and meaning.* Durham: Duke University Press, p. 6

The moment before can also be seen as an Apparatus.[9] The Apparatus or the moment before is not an instrument of passive observation but is part of shaping the shapes of the discourse and reality. The moment before is a material-discursive practice. When I speak about discourse I am not referring to a linguistic, semiotic practice or something that has been said (to think of discourse as merely spoken or written words forming a descriptive statement is to enact the mistake of representationalist thinking), but rather to what could have been said and the enabling of something that can be said or what counts as meaningful and create our perception, reality, and way of thinking.[10]

THE CONSISTENCY AND MATERIALITY OF THE MOMENT BEFORE

Identity secures itself through borders, exclusion, aggression, and projection, depending on the psychological needs of the body, its political intentions, knowledge, and meaning it wishes to create. What other domains, patterns, and dimensions could we experience if we let the trauma shapes lose their clear borders, their clear cuts, and clear fixed identities? Identity is the projection of the past on the idea of the future or a sense of belonging to a common past, but this perception sees the past as fixed and unable to change. It refuses to see the diffracted waves and patterns of the past and future that are active in creating the present. It reduces complexity to an expected pattern of behavior that will fit the frame of taxonomy and connects a social body that has lost its sense of solidarity and the feeling of responsibility, or, as Karen Barad put it, the ability to respond.

"Diffraction is not a set pattern, but rather an iterative (re)configuring of patterns of differentiating-entangling. As such, there is no moving beyond, no leaving the 'old' behind. There is no absolute boundary between here-now and there-then. There is nothing that is new; there is nothing that is not new. Matter itself is diffracted, dispersed, threaded through with materializing and sedimented effects of iterative reconfigurings of spacetimemattering, traces of what might yet (have) happen(ed)."[11]

Things receive meaning by how they are being connected, re-membered, and represented, and by whom. Meaning is established through connection of aesthetics, by the language that is used to talk about things, the memories, stories, and narratives that are being told about them, the emotions associated with them, the feelings that they evoke, the way we use them, how they are interpreted, classified, conceptualized, and the atmosphere or environment (Umwelt) it creates. All of this is based on traces and projections that are part of one's culture. When speaking about meaning, we speak about how epistemic knowledge is established, how it regulates and organizes our way of thinking, feeling, behaving, and acting. Meaning, ontology, and epistemology are inseparable from how culture is used to mark and maintain the discourses of identity and difference between groups.[12]

---

[9] When I speak about Apparatus I am referring to 2 notions of the Apparatus: To the Foucauldian apparatus, which are the various institutional, physical, and administrative mechanisms and knowledge structures which maintain the exercise of power within the social body and the discourse, or to Lyotard's notion of dispositifs, which indicate the connection, the relation in the libidinal web network. And to Karen Barad's notion of Apparatus: which are specific materials that not only emerge in time but can reconfigure memory and time-matter as part of the ongoing becoming of the world

[10] Foucault, M. (1989). *The archeology of knowledge.* London: Routledge

[11] Barad, K. (2014). *Diffracting diffraction: Cutting together-apart*, p. 1

[12] Hall, S. (1997). *Representation.* London: Sage

Time and memory create a space for the wounds to circulate. The wounds or traumas create a spatio-temporal space which I call the moment before. In my work I am using time, memory, and trauma as segments and an apparatus in order to create a fold in the discourse, the before and after, that are entangled, constantly diffracting and shapeshifting to create the present meaning.

CORRESPONDENCE AND MOVEMENT

In the moving images correspondence works that are created parallel to the theoretical research I am doing, the interview is used as a linguistic act that expresses a specific narrative. The battle is always over the narrative that constantly brings forth the voices of the hegemonic patriarchal narrative that tries to fix borders and identity, hiding behind a sense of stability, comfort, and security in the known shape of things and common sense as reality that it wishes to maintain.

My moving image correspondence practice is made from constant filming of my surroundings. Whether as a daily diary and moving image letter correspondence that I film with my phone while walking or cycling around, or through staged and premeditated situations which I film with a video camera; it is a permanent correspondence with shapes, movement, and space. *Often the works emerge from encounters that sneak in unexpectedly while walking around and filming. Later, when watching the materials and editing them, another way of wandering in space emerges, a different way of re-membering and moving in space-time becomes visible, noticeable, tangible.*

The moving image correspondence allows to embody and expose the multidirectional collapsing of time that exists in different shapes and forms that a landscape or a war zone is made from. These forms contain movement in time, space, memory, and oblivion. Through correspondence that moves between different space-time dimensions, one wanders or gets lost in a 'familiar landscape', in search of the unseen, that creates the most familiar shape(s). In the moving images correspondence dance a new order emerges, a re-membering of space and time that becomes graspable. It is a way to capture movement in space and its embodiment in the encounter. The moment before allows the trauma to manifest, circulate, take shape, and become part of the discourse through an act of correspondence. This correspondence enables the trauma to shapeshift the discourse, to bring in a personal trauma that will not unify or control the whole of the discourse; it will decenter the discourse and create a multidirectional space (with)in the discourse that will try to bring into the present moment an emotional connection to the future that is about to happen, in order to affect the moment before.[13]

A Dream (2020), the first part in this series of moving images correspondence with different entities, is an interview with a cactus that deals with the matter of the moment before the explosion. Through the video, I am trying to understand what this moment before the explosion is, what it is made from, what it consists of, its colors, sounds, rhythm, sensation, and the creation of atmosphere,

13
The term *multidirectional memory* was coined by Michael Rothberg in his book "Multidirectional Memory: Remembering the Holocaust in the Age of Decolonization" (2009) to conceptualize what happens when different histories of extreme violence confront each other in the public sphere. While the theory of multidirectional memory recognizes the struggles and contestations that accompany public articulations of memory, it seeks to understand how different struggles and memories can contribute to each other rather than competing in a zero-sum game on the place of remembrance. Here, in the context of this text, I am using the idea of multidirectional traumas that create a dispositif rather than compete with one another.

A Dream, video, 9:44 min (2020) Image from the video

shapes, and boundaries. It is not easy to capture this moment as often it is easier to recognize it in a retrospective; but if we look at the moment before also as an apparatus that sets each time a segment, that becomes the surface for the trauma to take hold and creates a landscape, we can try to work the moment before as a surface or discourses that not only lead to the explosion but also has the ability to change the event and the after-before. This changes the way the event/trauma unfolds, circulates, or changes circulation by understanding its shape and how a shape is created, and the effect of this shape in and on the landscape. The moment before enables the trauma to take shape and appear to us in space and time.

A Dream (2020) is a dialogue with a cactus that I brought from Italy for an experiment in the RCA sound studio. In the experiment, I tested the reaction of the cactus to the sound of an explosion.

I played a very loud explosion sound to the cactus while simultaneously recording the waves it emitted with a special ultrasonic microphone. I aimed to see if there is a change in its waves before and after the explosion. Before I started with the experiment I recorded an interview with it. In the interview, I told it what we were going to do and I also shared my doubts about it.

A Dream, video, 9:44 min (2020) Image from the video

I wanted to see if I could communicate with the Sabra, start a dialogue with it, and what it would mean to have a correspondence with a cactus. The video is an attempt to create an impossible dialogue with the cactus. It is an attempt to go outside the dimension of the familiar, of the seen reality that is known to us through our senses in an absurd and humoristic act that tries to sit with the trauma and its aggressiveness in the same space. It is not about trying to work out the trauma in a practice of a psychoanalytic conversation, but rather giving it a space to present and embody itself, to create a certain sensual space and atmosphere in a discourse that tries to silence it. The video is a poetic act that attempts to work out different traumas of war of different generations and entities that share history. Although some of these entities in the video did not physically experience some of the events, they still embodied the memory traces of these events.

The work also explores the idea of putting something in a sterile room or laboratory that is completely separate from its surroundings, its trace, and shape that makes it in an attempt to obtain an objective result that stands for itself. The work questions the existence of a sterile space as an empty page, tabula rasa. It questions that shape has no trace of trauma and memory that influences it; rather, it is embodied in the language and matter, which are already active in the encounter that creates it. In the video, I am looking at the moment before in order to understand how it serves as a surface or ground zero, that enables the trauma to take hold and is inseparable from our experience. How the past is projected into the future, returning to create the now, solidifying the trauma, situating it, and letting it dwell and recirculate. The human and non-human matter is memory that diffracts and creates the world. Memory is time that life has encoded in material, shapes, and forms that contain movement, and this movement in time becomes the present and future meaning.

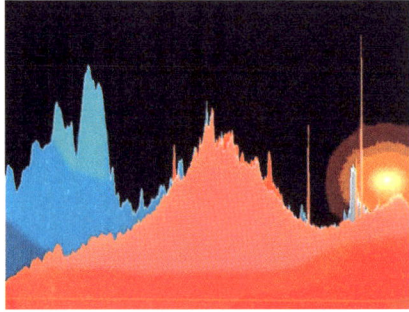

A Dream, video, 9:44 min (2020) Image from the video

Ultrasonic waves cannot be heard by the human ear, but we can see their visual representation and the changes in them. I placed the blue sound wave of my voice and the red ultrasonic wave of the cactus on top of each other, in order to create a visual dialogue, a landscape of a dialogue that interacts in the moment before the explosion. An existence in which the two waves matter and create a different reality; the two events are placed together so both voices can be heard, and neither one of them is pushed into the realm of the 'invisible'.

The three protagonists (cacti, human, and tank) are haunted by the explosion in some way or another and are part of the overall fluid environment that creates that kind of weird shapeshifting that I am looking at in order to understand and shed a light on how trauma takes shape, diffracts, and creates our landscape, perception, and atmosphere. The encounter in my works is not about meeting the Sabra or the tank, the act of materiality of the correspondence itself is the encounter. A multidirectional encounter that enables engagement with the trauma and the discourse that allows it to enter our ability to grasp it.

In order to understand trauma or try to work out a trauma, we need to understand and recognize the shape of trauma, its pattern, and the effect it creates. Without doing so, one cannot recognize and fight the mechanisms at play that try to silence the trauma and stop it from flowing and entering a certain shape that will enable it to become present in the discourse. The moment before leads to a certain discourse and is the discourse itself, that contains the moment after and the before at the same time and can be re-membered in different ways. Art or a poetic act is an encounter that has the ability to do so; that is why often art is the first to be targeted or attacked. Art can allow the energy to go into different shapes and bring the unseen shapes into visibility. Energy is not committed to a specific shape and can flow in and out of shapes, shapeshift forms and patterns, and by doing so it can subvert the hegemonic linguistic narrative that might not even recognize it as such, as sometimes it had no presence in the commonly known discourse up to that point. The silenced energy and or the silenced trauma create an encounter between the verbal and non-verbal language.[14] This encounter creates a space that exposes the seams of the symbolic order and power structure.[15] This moment creates an opportunity, a space for the re-membering to take place. The possibility of a re-membering of matter of past and future through art, into a new shape, a new dimension, a new order of space-time that comes to presence and takes space in the discourse, that will have the ability to affect and maybe even change the discourse (even if only in tiny bits) and allow us to sit with the trauma in the same space.

14
Lyotard, J.-F. (2011 [1971]). *Discourse, figure*. Minneapolis: University of Minnesota Press. Translated by Antony Hudek & Mary Lydon

15
Sharpe, C. (2016). *In the wake: On blackness and being*. Durham: Duke University Press

Marie Kammler
Strollology as a State of Mind
An Aesthetic Approach and Intervention to Pedestrian Centred Urban Planning

After decades of urban planning in the favour of cars, we can see that city centres do not have much in common with liveable areas where one would like to spend time or invite children to play safely. The roads are on the verge of collapsing under the number of motorists and still shop windows tend to remain empty more and more often.

In Palermo, young people living in the surrounding residential areas rather decide to stay home in the evening than being stuck for hours in the endless traffic jams[1] on their way to the next bar. The mayor of Stuttgart claimed in 2017 that the cities' transport sector was about to collapse because of massive individual motor car traffic. Many people express their wish to have a better infrastructure such as more public parks and green spaces[2], more liveability and public spaces where they are not obliged to purchase anything – challenges well known in urban areas around the globe. And still, there is a dissonance between the belief that city centres are dependent on individual motor car traffic and cars being allowed to drive everywhere on the one hand and the rising awareness that cities with large pedestrian areas are more attractive to spend one's time on the other hand. Many city centres are flooded by motorised private transport. That is why many cities decide to discuss the topic of liveable urban areas. New concepts of urban planning are needed.

The city of Barcelona, to mention a positive example, has become very popular by starting the realization of the so-called Superblocks (Superillas) concept[3] in 1993. In 2013, the city introduced the project in the course of the "2013–2018 Urban Mobility Plan of Barcelona" as "a government-funded project identifying 120 intersections to be converted" into liveable pedestrian centred places and "to recover space for the community, improve biodiversity, move towards sustainable mobility, and encourage social cohesion".[4] In the upcoming years, the city plans to transform many more intersections into Superblocks.

The city of Vienna instead started its pedestrian centred approach to the design of the city centre already in the 1960.[5] In 1968, big parts of the streets in the inner city were transformed into pedestrian areas which, in the beginning, did not appeal to many people but today, Vienna's citizens are proud of moving around by foot one third of their daily routes.[6] Interestingly, many of these thoughts have been relevant about forty years ago already, but still cities have continuously been planned in the non-pedestrian friendly way we are experiencing today.

One theorist who addressed these challenges was Lucius Burckhardt; he developed a practice in the 1990ies that can contribute to these challenges significantly: "Spaziergangswissenschaft" in German, "the Science of Strollology" in English. In the following, I will give some insights into Burckhardt's work and reflect on his theories, setting them in contrast to contemporary human-centred approaches in urban planning. In this way, 'walking' will be examined in three steps: As a *performative form of urban criticism*, as a *way to shift perception*, and finally as a *pedagogical concept*.

[1] URL: https://www.palermo-today.it/cronaca/palermo-citta-piu-traffico-italia-tom-tom-2021.html

[2] URL: https://www.fussverkehrskongress.de/rueckblick-2020/#-mediathek

[3] URL: www.citiesforum.org/news/superblock-superilla-barcelona-a-city-redefined/

[4] ibid.

[5] URL: www.spiegel.de/spiegel/autos-in-innenstaedten-wir-haben-systematisch-stau-erzeugt-a-1196234.html

[6] URL: www.wienzufuss.at/zu-fuss-gehen-in-zahlen/

THE SCIENCE OF STROLLOLOGY

Lucius Burckhardt was born in 1952 in Davos and has a background in sociology and economics. After working in various positions between Switzerland and Germany, he received a professorship for socio-economics of urban systems at Gesamthochschule Kassel in 1973. There, he founded the Science of Strollology together with his wife and artist Annemarie Burckhardt.[7]

At its core, the Science of Strollology is not about the walk one might take during leisure time. More so, as Lucius Burckhardt puts it, "(t)he Science of Strollology addresses something completely different from the traditional stroll. It is a caricature of that role model. It has inherited the leisurely *flâneur's* distance from reality but has nonetheless a nostalgic tenor. Strollology was created out of the sense of irony – because there are many things today one can regard only with irony."[8] One of these things for Burckhardt certainly is the car-centred planning of post-war cities in Europe. New infrastructures and mobility allow quick movement but, at the same time, a loss of connection to the very environment one is traversing. Or, as Burckhardt states, "Strollology examines the sequences in which a person perceives his[*her] surroundings. For it is not as we find ourselves 'beamed' all of a sudden to Piccadilly Circus or Cancelleria; instead we find our ways there, one way or another".[9] And further on: "We are interested in the walk not as a means of representation, but rather as a mode of perception."[10] For the Burckhardts the method of walking is especially about the site-specific experiences and details one is able to notice through this slow and highly conscious way of moving. In this spirit, Annemarie and Lucius Burckhardt created a wide range of experiments and urban interventions to reflect on man-made environments. Especially about the crucial details one is able to grasp by walking consciously through the particular environments instead of using motorised ways of mobility. *Walking in this context is one of their critical aesthetic practices for research and public debate.* In their perspective, such aesthetic approaches can even serve to mediate between different points of view and facilitate communication about possible futures: "Certain perspectives can probably be conveyed by art alone, since the human gaze is limited in so many ways nowadays that people are scarcely able to step back and even realise it. Art alone is able to communicate this without being preachy or hurtful. With our walks, we switch off peoples fear of the unknown. And we have fun, too."[11]

Until today, the concept of Strollology has a strong connection to the city of Kassel in Germany. Not only is there a public place on the university's campus called *Lucius Burckhardt Platz*, where the students' union executive committee offers a workshop and support for self-repairing bicycles. In addition, there is an endowed professorship called the *Annemarie und Lucius Burckhardt Professur* at the local art academy, which makes sure that Burckhardt's critiques and approaches find their way into the students' curriculum also today.

[7] Fezer, J., & Schmitz, M. (Eds.). (2012). *Lucius Burckhardt writings: Rethinking man-made environments. Politics, landscape & design.* Wien: Springer-Verlag, p. 281

[8] Burckhardt, L. (2000). Strollology: A minor subject. In conversation with Hans Ulrich Obrist. In M. Ritter & M. Schmitz (Eds.), *Why is landscape beautiful? The science of strollology.* Basel: Birkhäuser, p. 11

[9] Burckhardt, L. (1996). Strollological observations on perception of the environment and the task facing our generation. In M. Ritter & M. Schmitz (Eds.), *Why is landscape beautiful? The science of strollology.* Basel: Birkhäuser, p. 225

[10] Burckhardt, L. (1995). The science of strollology. In M. Ritter & M. Schmitz (Eds.), *Why is landscape beautiful? The science of strollology.* Basel: Birkhäuser, p. 231

[11] Burckhardt, 2000, p. 9

[12] In English "Lucius Burckhardt Square"

However, not only the university still honours its former professor and the pedagogical concepts he developed together with his wife; another very well-known example is the international exhibition for contemporary art, *documenta*, which takes place in Kassel every five years. In its 14th edition, the Science of Strollology received a lot attention, especially in the field of art education. In that year, the established concept of guided tours of the exhibited artworks was transformed into non-hierarchical "walks" across the exhibition sites with the aim of exchange of knowledge.[13] Together with an art mediator, the groups visited the exhibition venues and reflected on the pieces bringing together all of the group's knowledge, perspectives, questions and experiences. This way, every tour had the potential to be highly unique and create new insights.

[13] URL: www.documenta14.de/de/public-education

These examples illustrate how Strollology can enter research and educational settings. In fact, many of the strollological aspects can be transferred to other contexts. Especially the conscious change of speed in movement and perception as well as the body-focused interventions play a major role and form the particular approach of Strollology.

In the following section, I will present three of Burckhardt's interventions, which serve as examples for three core aspects: Strolling *as a performative form of urban criticism* portrays Burckhardt's approach of aesthetic interventions in public space highlighting serious deficits in the field of urban planning. Secondly, *strolling as a way to shift perception* describes how the act of walking can generate new perspectives and how the experiences made can be used as a base to rethink the ways urban environments should be designed – and whom they should serve in future. The third aspect is *strolling as a pedagogical concept* which summarises the way Lucius Burckhardt engaged his students into specific interventions and set frames for learning that involved a physical experience to reflect on human-made environments. Although the following paragraphs will highlight these specific perspectives, they should not be understood as detached from each other. Rather, they are different aspects of Burckhardt's oeuvre interwoven with each other.

THE ZEBRA CROSSING – STROLLING AS PERFORMATIVE URBAN CRITICISM

"The premise for the city walks is that we no longer really see our everyday surroundings. Urban dwellers' quality of life has been whittled away in a process so gradual it was barely perceptible. When the number of cars increased, the street ceased to be an area one might play in."[14] *"Then zebra crossings*[15] *were installed and people were happy to be able at least to cross the street in safety. This (loss of the street and public space) basically constitutes a permanent expropriation but we fail to perceive it as such and may even regard it as beneficial, since we appear to gain something in return. The zebra crossing is safe and secure, they say, but in fact we should be able to cross any road safely, anywhere. And over time, the zebra crossing itself comes to be regarded as unsafe and is replaced by a set of traffic lights at which one must wait for a signal before crossing. This expropriation always takes place bit by bit, so we cannot easily see and experience the total loss."*[16]

[14] Burckhardt, L. (1993). A matter of looking and recognizing. In conversation with Thomas Fuchs. In M. Ritter & M. Schmitz (Eds.), *Why is landscape beautiful? The science of strollology.* Basel: Birkhäuser, p. 284

[15] "British term for pedestrian crosswalks marked with white stripes", ibid., p. 284

[16] Burckhardt, 1993, p. 284

This observation and critique on the non-pedestrian-friendly changes in urban planning illuminates how pedestrian crossings were created in the name of security but ended up reducing flexibility of choosing one's individual path through the city. In 1993, Burckhardt transformed this into a performative social experiment in Kassel. Together with his students and artist Gerhard Lang, Lucius Burckhardt chose a centrally located multi-lane road, where they temporarily installed a huge portable zebra striped carpet (made by Lang) across all six lanes and together walked across the street at any selected spot. Obviously, the performative act interrupted the traffic by blocking its normal velocity and cars. This action gave rise to a public discussion on the topic of "the disappropriation of city dwellers' right to walk"[17], that involved blocked motorists as well as passers-by. The aesthetic intervention and the very visible act of walking created an immediate experience, able to propel people to reflect critically on certain structural conditions in our built environments. For Burckhardt, walking is a matter of looking and recognising: "City walks – such as the 'ZEBRA crossing', the one we staged in Kassel city centre – are intended to convey this specific insight, insight into what we have lost."[18] The recognition of what has been lost through the car-friendly planning of the city centre is easy: "The subject in this case is the road network. The shopping street network is lost to us now. It has ceded to the pedestrian strip of Obere Königsstraße, with all the economic repercussion this entails for property values, store rents and the range of available goods."[19] On the basis of this example, Burckhardt reflects the performative *ZEBRA-crossing-walk* on various levels: Firstly, on the pedestrians' (im-)possibility to cross the road wherever they prefer and the structurally built hierarchies between road users. Secondly, he concludes the aftermath of the car-friendly urban planning generated for the whole city centre: Being locked-in between several multi-lane highways that create a concentration of retail spaces in a contrastingly small radius.

[17] Fezer, J., & Schmitz, M. (Eds.). (2012). *Lucius Burckhardt writings: Rethinking man-made environments. Politics, landscape & design.* Wien: Springer-Verlag, p. 245

[18] Burckhardt, 1993, p. 285

[19] ibid.

157

Das Zebra streifen, Kassel 1993
Foto: Angela Siever
© Martin Schmitz Verlag

Autofahrerspaziergang, Kassel 1993
Seminar Wahrnehmung und Verkehr
Foto: Bertram Weisshaar
© Martin Schmitz Verlag

MOVING FRAMES – STROLLING AS A WAY TO SHIFT PERCEPTION

"Another action of ours served to reproduce the view through a windshield but in an alienated form, without the usual protective surrounding of a car. We made portable windscreens from transparent plastic sheets then marched two-by-two along a stretch of slip road (the Frankfurter Strasse on the Weinberg), spread out so as to block the road. There is no sidewalk beside this stretch of road, only a brick wall, and hence no safe place to dodge the traffic. The experience is difficult to describe. The motorist's usual sense of safety evaporated. The danger felt immediate. Not that we had exposed ourselves to any real danger here, since a police car followed our parade. Our acute sense of danger therefore appears all the more remarkable."[20]

[20] Burckhardt, 1995, p. 262

[21] Burckhardt, 2000, p. 8

The windshield-walk, which Lucius Burckhardt later on described as the most impressive experimental walk for himself, aimed to generate a literal change of the 'framing' of perception. Together with a group of students, they "aimed to reproduce the motorists' perspective"[21] and reflected on what impressions that experience produced for the participants. The interesting point to see is that, although most of them actually were motorists and had taken the road before, the reduction of speed and protection during the walk triggered a fundamental change in perception. Suddenly, the participants were able to look left and right, to realise the lack of a sidewalk, the difference between protected and unprotected users; they experienced how wide the road actually is and felt the inherent feeling of danger of this environment. A rare experience to have.

This experimental stroll shows how the Burckhardt's oftentimes used the method of walking as an aesthetic approach to embody theoretical problems and make them tangible. In this case the major theme was: "What do we experience through a windshield?"[22] And the experience comes with the fact, that "we are no longer really conscious of how windshields limit our perception".[23] "One mainly looks straight ahead when driving a car. One is compelled to take that perspective. But one doesn't even realise it until one begins to think about perspective."[24] Thinking about perspectives and making them tangible through physical interventions that shift the framing of one's perception is a major part of the Burckhardts' pedagogical concept.

22 ibid.

23 ibid.

24 ibid.

STROLLING AS A PEDAGOGICAL CONCEPT

The Burckhardts' approach of walking as an aesthetical method to reflect on critical matters was an important component of the education of aspiring architects and urban planners at Kassel University at that time. During their period at Kassel University (1972–1997), the Burckhardts developed a multitude of experimental walks that were vitalising certain questions of planning instead of focusing only on the theoretical aspects.

"Our seminars, insofar as they address the city, seek to render visible that which is actually and generally available and visible but which urban dwellers apparently now fail to perceive (...) Our approach – the 'action teaching' focus [sic] on taking a scientific stroll together – put [sic] some life back onto the issue. It is to be hoped that the participants will remember their view of such strolls in the future (...)."[25]

25 Burckhardt, 1995, p. 261

In all of their walks, the Burckhardts created a strong relation between built environments and the physical impression one can only experience as a pedestrian. They focused on the consequences a car-centric urban planning generates and, in this way, created a strong practical and theoretical base for future planning.

FROM CAR-CENTRIC TO PEOPLE-CENTRIC CITIES

Reading Lucius Burckhardt's texts and descriptions from a contemporary perspective, it seems hard to believe that today, decades later, our cities seem to have learned so little. Still, there are too many cars in the city centres – even more than in those days. Still, there are six-lane highways creating unbreachable barriers in city centres cutting one quarter from another. Still, there are people of all ages living close to these roads suffering the noise and pollution and wishing for more green space to meet or play.

As mentioned in the beginning, in the last years something like a movement with a focus on people and pedestrian-centred urban areas has formed around the globe. More and more cities dare to try out conferring the rights to use areas formerly utilised as parking sites or residential streets differently. Many times, these experiments start 'from

Raamwerk: Freiluftexperiment Untere Königsstraße, Kassel 2021
Foto: Sinah Hackenberg
©Raamwerk e.V.

below'; they are developed by initiatives and groups of urban dwellers and architects, designers, sociologists, ecologists, economists etc. wanting to turn the streets into a more liveable space than what it is today.

FREILUFTEXPERIMENT UNTERE KÖNIGSSTRASSE

The Freiluftexperiment Untere Königsstraße[25] is one recent example of an experimental approach for such a transformation; it was created by the social design studio Raamwerk[26] together with the city council and many other local stakeholders in the city of Kassel.

At present, Königsstraße in Kassel is divided into two parts: Obere Königsstraße[27] is the main shopping strip for the big chains and a pedestrian area since ages, whereas Untere Königsstraße[28] is shaped by international supermarkets and rather low-priced culinary offers. Both parts of the street are cut by a six-lane crossroad (Am Stern), which makes it challenging for pedestrians to pass from one side to the other. Also, Untere Königsstraße is still open for cars to drive through. As a consequence, thousands of cars and trucks take this strip of few hundred meters as a shortcut through the city centre every day. This again entails high pollution and noise for the residents, limited space for outdoor seating areas for the restaurants, and is per se a dangerous setting for kids and families. Interestingly, this strip of Untere Königsstraße is located between two of the Burckhardts' domains: The campus of Kassel University on the one side and the six-lane road where the ZEBRA crossing intervention took place on the other side, to highlight the non-human-friendly design of the road through the performative walk and the temporary blocking of the whole street.

[25] Literally: Experiment in the urban open space "Untere Königsstrasse" (street name)

[26] URL: www.raamwerk.de

[27] The upper part of the road

[28] The lower part of the road

The Freiluftexperiment Untere Königsstraße[29] refers to this intervention and to Burckhardt's Strollology in general: During the project, the lower part of the street was turned into a pedestrian area for one month during which the four-lane road was closed for motorists and gave space to a new zonal structure. The pedestrian walk way – which had always been overcrowded, because it was shared between pedestrians, displayed fruit, terrace chairs and people walking their bikes due to the traffic – was given to the shop owners to display their goods or build an outdoor seating area. Still, public transport was allowed to drive in the very centre of the street but left and right – where motorists used to have the authority – a shared zone for pedestrians, cyclists, skateboarders and playing kinds was created, each of them taking care for the others. The emerging space was designed to be a zone for encounter – encounter between people from different backgrounds, ages or political views on the world in general and on cities and urban planning in specific.

[29] URL: www.freiluft-experiment.de

A major part of the design of this transformative process was to include the local stakeholders and residents not only accessing their own resources but also by co-organising a number of cultural impulses and interventions that focused on the newly gained space for pedestrians and the new roles that came along with it. One aim was to 'force' people to slow down in their daily routes from A to B and let them perceive this part of the street as a neighbourhood and as a place for people, or to experience the street from a new perspective that usually is exclusive to cars. And with these new impressions in mind perhaps to rethink how this street could be used in the future. And even further, to think about how cities could be designed in the future.

The idea was to make the vision of a transformed Königstraße tangible. Interestingly, during the first days of the car-free road and even after the first weeks one was clearly able to see how deep the fear of the street was still a embodied memory by all the adult pedestrians: Even though motorists had no access and the road was explicitly there to walk on, many people avoided moving there 'unprotectedly'. People would rather walk their way through the newly set up terraces of local restaurants than make their way onto the former highway. This phenomenon of an 'embodied fear of the street' and the strong feeling of danger one is experiencing very much goes along with the sensations Burckhardt describes in the context of the windshield walk: "The experience is difficult to describe. The motorist's usual sense of safety evaporated. The danger felt immediate. Not that we had exposed ourselves to any real danger here (…). Our acute sense of danger therefore appears all the more remarkable."[30]

[30] Burckhardt, 1995, p. 263

Raamwerk's role as initiator to that effect was the design of a participative process to generate the public programme and the relational design of the intervention. Through their community-oriented approach and focus on the local resources, the stakeholders such as pedestrians, shop owners, bikers etc. were invited to participate shaping the experiment. The aim was to reduce the abstraction of the potential that the street area could contain and to make the vision more tangible. In this sense, the approach of a tactical urbanism allowed people to make their own experiences with the ideas and thus render the formerly abstract futures way more thinkable. Many participants described how their perception of the space changed over the course of the temporary focus on pedestrians. Through their aesthetic intervention, Raamwerk paved the way to the point of a political decision and a long-term transformation of the street from below, together with the people on site. Still, these changes are only slowly taking root and the city has still a long way to go until the street suits the inhabitants' needs. This recent aesthetic approach of working with the pedestrians' experience to discuss relevant topics in urban planning reminds of Lucius Burckhardt saying, "art allows to 'switch off' people's fear of the unknown"[31]

A zebra-striped carpet temporarily placed on a street with high traffic to stage a performative crossing, the shifted perception of the city through a windshield as a 'walking motorist', the exclusion of motor-driven vehicles in a busy street, to give space to pedestrians – all the projects certainly offer an insight of what Burckhardt wanted to create with his Science of Strollology: To elicit aesthetic and embodied experiences and to discuss the potentials of a road designed according to the needs of urban dwellers and residents. Still, one important connecting aspect is the reduced speed in moving as a base for perception, problem analysis and ideation. Not only 'walking' as movement but the attention to putting oneself physically into a specific situation seems to open up new perspectives on urban mobility as the described projects illuminate.

[31] Burckhardt, 2000, p. 9

The challenges many city centres are or will be facing in the upcoming years will need pedestrian-centered approaches since processes of transformation in urban areas are concerning a wide range of stakeholders, their acceptance to the new approaches will be indispensable. As this article might have shown, the Burckhardts' Science of Strollology can serve as an impulse to a more human-centred urban planning: Reducing speed, leaving the protecting capsules of cars that also form our perceptive patterns, and putting one's own body into the very environment in discussion, observing and igniting processes that change habituated perceptions, reflecting together, and framing the needs. In short, strollology is an approach for making ideas tangible and creating frames to try out possible futures.

Maja Maksimović, Darija Medić & Mirjana Utvić

Notes in Public Space: Inscribing the Pavement, Annotating the City

This text was created within the project *Wondering Women*, the aim of which was to provoke traditional academic epistemology and writing and engage in an investigation of the city of Belgrade, entangling bodies and learning by being in the world that opens itself to sensorial experiences, creating time/space together with our memories, scars, city textures and imagination.[1] With the addition of Denver as a city on a different continent and context, it is a continuation of explorations of urban landscapes and bodying of streets which are its main research unit. We base our research on the practice of flânerie, the act of "strolling" through urban spaces, but we do not position ourselves as distant and lone spectators, the attitude that belongs to an emblematic figure of the flâneur.[2] Although women were traditionally excluded from public space and were the object of observation rather than observers, we postulate that the identity of the flâneuse does not solely signify women who wander the streets but involves quite a different presence than the one that was attributed to the flâneur. There is no separation between the subject and object of knowing; wandering is a creative act of coming into existence by merging, discovering, preserving, and (re)valuating the city spaces that have been taken for granted, pushed aside, forgotten, or neglected. We are witnesses of the existence of the material, its position, we value it, compare it, evaluate it, describe it, and sense it. However, these actions of flâneurs could also possibly turn into a colonization of space. For example, today's investment building politics of housing where profit rules can be seen as a type of wandering colonization of different culturally and historically important districts like Dorćol, Vračar, and Zemun in Belgrade but also Pančevo, Novi Banovci, and other settlements near the capital of Serbia, a formerly socialist country now adopting neoliberal trends from the West. Investors unintentionally take the role of wanderers in search of deprived, 'undiscovered', unpopular, domestic city areas that could be transformed into commercial spaces. However, over time, what once made these neighborhoods desirable for investments disappears after they are co-opted. Signature urbanism, architecture, volumetric quality of space, lifestyle, and communities that it supported and nurtured are gone.

In this paper, we will present three ways of wandering following Quennau's "exercises in style" (Quennau, 1981)[3] and build into experimental inquiries into and involvement with tactical traces in public space. Stemming from our diverse but overlapping disciplinary homes, we question what traces can be made visible, be imagined visible, and what can be their effect depending on the positionality, authorship, and location of the trace through three narrative openings. The exercises rethink the current contextual affordances of anonymity in light of agency, privilege, and accountability in public discourse. They rethink the affordances of traces as grand gestures of the genius author versus traces of need, expression as overcoming discomfort, and practicing agency. How can the city be read and annotated with notes on the margins of its writings? In doing so, the exercises involve the principles of data feminism in conversation with sensual scholarship[4] in breaking the binary either-or of rationalist (commonly projected as masculinist) versus romanticist (commonly projected as feminine) perceptions of knowledge. In other words, this research

[1] Maksimovic, M., Joksimović, J., & Utvić, M. (2020). Haptic exploration of urban Belgrade – Uniting female gazes through the projec Wa(o)ndering Women. *Revista Educação, Artes e Inclusão, 16*(4), 216–241

[2] Rizk, J., & Birioukov, A. (2017). Following the flâneur: The methodological possibilities and applications of flânerie in new urban spaces. *The Qualitative Report, 22*(12), 3268–3286

[3] ibid.

[4] Stoller, P. (2010). *Sensuous scholarship*. Philadelphia: University of Pennsylvania Press

is a practice in decentering and recuperating spaces from analytical epistemic violence[5] to include perspectival and participatory knowing[6], not as an exotic, but as a thoroughly present and actively ignored factor in cognition. By embarking on a quest to inscribe the positionality of the flâneuse, these exercises take on the role of bodily presence in public space as an uncovering of "wild facts".[7]

How does data become feminist in the map of a city? How is street data embodied through visceralization? How does societal vulnerability affect the experience of public spaces? How can politics of inscription be negotiated, evaluated, and reconfigured from one's particular positionality?

The three exercises offer three distinct perspectives spoken from the body, (per-)forming knowledge spaces from corporeal involvement in its immediate surroundings.

[5] Spivak, G. C. (1998). Can the subaltern speak? In C. Nelson & L. Grossberg (Eds.), *Marxism and the interpretation of culture.* Urbana: University of Illinois Press

[6] Vervaeke, J., Lillicrap, T. P., & Richards, B. A. (2012). Relevance realization and the emerging framework in cognitive science. *Journal of Logic and Computation, 22*(1), 79–99

[7] Terranova, F. (Director). (2016). *Donna Haraway: Storytelling for earthly survival* [Documentary film]

LIMINAL SPACES OF BROADWAY
DARIJA

In search of clarity in situating my knowledge and forming awareness of my positionality, I surrendered to the act of walking as an act of speculative inquiry in a classical appropriation of the flâneur and by entering a Temporary Autonomous Zone[8]: Walking unnoticed in one's city, in someone else's city, in another country, as an immigrant with an unmistakable accent from Slavic Eastern Europe, socialized in a deficit narrative, yet an affluent participant of the higher education chain, one that is notorious for inducing chronic anxiety disorders among its populations. In thinking of my unearned privileges and my taking up space in this particular street, I ask myself: Which bodies are allowed to experience a stroll, here, at this moment? The flâneur embows a preexisting state of liberation, on the opposite side of trauma.

[8] Bey, H. (1991). T.A.Z.: *The temporary autonomous zone, ontological anarchy, poetic terrorism.* New York: Autonomedia

1

2

Images
1: Abandoned mask, courtesy of the global pandemic, November 2021, South Broadway, Denver
2: Abandoned bottle of whiskey
3: Abandoned person covered with a blanket on South Broadway, Denver, November 2021
4: Closed business on South Broadway, Denver, November 2021
5: The homeless as exiled wanderers (left: August 2021, right: November 2021), South Broadway, Denver

The scene of inquiry is the vibrant street of Broadway in Denver, Colorado. Yet, there is an effort in guiding attention to the small, unmeasurable signifiers of transitioning, of change. This space is a diary of performing mapping while not leaving objects and traces in public space, realized through the seemingly but hardly innocent act of documenting scenes as snapshots in time. Some of them mark the era of still being in a global pandemic after a year and a half, of still grappling with public policies, of tossing masks in protest and venues closing. Finished bottles of whiskey. Temporary settlements of the eternally expelled, the never digital nomads: the homeless. Yet, Christmas is approaching.

THE CHANGING, THE UNPROFITABLE, THEREFORE NON-VALUABLE

The accumulation of byproducts is a tracing of the urban landscape that speaks a story of layers, archives, of building on top of preexisting states. Inscribing can never come as a blank slate on the streets of a city.[9] In that way, the decision for the act of tracing in this exercise in style was to create a documentation, an anarchival process.[10] The nature of byproducts is also a marker of liminality, the consequences of the temporality of the spaces in between. This mapping comes into being as an active process, always unfolding, always subjective, always small scale, always discriminating, always painting an intentional picture, always carrying unintentional aspects which could be completely different from day to day. Unlike the reductionism of flattening data into a citywide representation, this map follows a part of a street, one which the subject researcher is in close contact with, not extracted from. One which stems from a lived knowledge of a particular positionality and perspective, deeply embodied and accountable to its biases and fragmentary nature of the multiplicity of partial perspectives[11], opposite from the detached gaze of the conventional flâneur. One which is not cleansed into 'pure' data, but additionally skewed in the act of mediating the end perspective, leveraging the widely available practice of filtering images as a tool of obfuscation and protection of anonymity.

The act of tracing with a camera has demonstrated in itself to be an experiential marker of presence to other passers-by, directing their attention to the tracer (me), as well as to the object of tracing (the signifiers of transitionality). The meaning of the scene is left unexamined from the perspective of the bypassers, to maintain the space of meaning-making from the experiential. Yet, the shift of attention of the flâneuse has marked an effect on the immediate surrounding of daily habituation in public space. As such it provokes the question: Can the space of the flâneuse function as an intervention to disintegrate the disinterest of the flâneur into creating spaces of shared co-liberation?[12] And how can accountability find a place in the act of reproducing the documented through developing intentional lensing, protecting subjectivities in public space?

[9] Mattern, S. (2017). *Code and clay, data and dirt: Five thousand years of urban media.* Minneapolis: University of Minnesota Press

[10] Zielinski, S., & Winthrop-Young, G. (2015). Anarcheology for anarchives: Why do we need – especially for the arts – a complementary concept to the archive? *Journal of Contemporary Archaeology, 2*(1), 116–125

[11] D'Ignazio, C., & Klein, L. F. (2020). *Data feminism.* Cambridge: MIT Press

[12] ibid.

BELGRADE – A LIQUID CITY
MAJA

The water finds its way. Inspired by the fascination with the rain – and Mirjana's suggestion – I followed the rain in the city, and tried to wander by following the traces of water. I was intrigued with the softness that rain created by changing the city texture, the light, and bringing new sounds and rhythms. With those sounds, I could experience materials around me and become aware that I myself am made of wet matter. The fluidity of my being merged with water-soaked streets. My emotional meltdown is mirrored in the ponds. However, that water does not flow. It accumulates and disappears. Its ephemerality allows for my personal flow and leakage. I feel like I am overflowing the so-called limits of my body. Sweat and rain mix on my skin, everything appears salty. The firm boundaries of the city have softened, the ground has become muddy, everything is moving. My cells and molecules. The masculine structure of the city is disturbed.

The body is often phenomenologically absent in everyday life and the relationship with the body is seen as unproblematic, which gives us the freedom to be and act. "Our bodies are highly articulated, yet in a state of (continuous) disappearance."[13] In that line of thought, Ann Marie Mol[14] conceives of the body not as a singular, limited entity, bounded by skin, but speaks of bodies that expand and connect with other human and non-human bodies, practices, technologies, and objects. And Stacey Alaimo[15] introduces the concept of trans-corporeality, thus emphasizing the porosity of the body and the belief that beings are intertwined with the dynamic, material world that passes through them, transforms them, and thus itself changes. In an effort to overcome the binary separation of culture and nature, the author provokes the subject of Western humanistic individualism – which imagines itself as transcendent, disembodied and removed from the world it explores – arguing that we need a new, more potent and complex understanding of matter.[16] Simply put, this concept implies the interconnectedness and exchange between the human body and life and inanimate nature. The substances of humanity are inseparable from the environment.[17] The idea of the processes and porosity of the body relies on the approach of the new materialism according to which the body is constantly evolving; it is not an isolated and independent self-regulating entity but a multiple matter that is produced in action with the environment. That matter is not limited by facts, it is not mutable or passive, nor is it a fixed support, location, referent, or source of sustainability for discourse.[18]

13
Bendelow, G. A., & Williams, S. J. (2002). *The lived body: Sociological themes, embodied issues*. London: Routledge

14
Mol, A. M. (2003). *The body multiple*. Durham: Duke University Press

15
Alaimo, S. (2010). *Bodily natures: Science, environment, and the material self*. Bloomington: Indiana University Press

16
Alaimo, S. (2018). Trans-corporeality. In R. Braidotti & M. Hlavajova (Eds.), *Posthuman glossary*. London: Bloomsbury, 435–438

17
Alaimo, 2010

18
Barad, K. (2007). *Meeting the universe halfway: Quantum physics and the entanglement of matter and meaning*. Durham: Duke University Press

The transcorporeal subject is generated and intertwined with biological, technological, economic, social, political, and other systems, processes and events, in different scales.[19] The assumption underlying this view of the body is that materials are not inert. In this paper, we do not view the body as socio-constructivist (materiality shaped by the action of vectors of social relations), but we understand (and experience) it in the interaction of its agency and living and non-living agents. The matter is not fixed, determined, and unchangeable, but active. Schilling points out that, although the body is influenced by discourse, the question remains how it reacts and affects the discourses that shape it.[20]

Being bodies of water our borders are open and vulnerable[21] and we are constantly shaping and reshaping, and in this fluidity connect with other bodies and worlds. "The bodies from which we siphon and into which we pour ourselves are certainly other human bodies (a kissable lover, a blood transfused stranger, a nursing infant), but they are just as likely a sea, a cistern, an underground reservoir of once-was-rain".[22] When this connection disappears, I leak. Liquid is inscribed in the materiality of the streets and buildings as it finds cracks it can get into. Filled with water, those ruptures become visible. My cracks are visible. They are dirty and hollow.

19
Alaimo, 2018

20
Shilling, C. (1993). *The body and social theory.* London: Sage

21
Neimanis, A. (2017). *Bodies of water: Posthuman feminist phenomenology.* New York: Bloomsbury Academic

22
ibid., p. 2

PLAYFULNESS OF WANDERMENT MIRJANA

Wandering comes naturally, like the need to play. The excitement of changing track has never been a burden, a loss, a fear – to change tracks to make *detours* as something catches my sight, something miraculous, new, mysterious, unknown and exciting to my senses – was always a treat of a discovery.

Curiosity, this feeling of desperately wanting to know what is behind, over there, who lives there, is there more, does it smell, can I touch it – overwhelms me in my deliberate or not wanderments around Belgrade, especially. I would sneak into a place to observe, to touch, to find out and discover all those secret lives hidden, kept behind closed or not closed doors. Gently, I would come in and wonder who lives there, what traces of their lives could be found. Will someone come and yell at me asking *'Who are you and why are you inside?'* – and I imagine my answer would be something like: *'The doors were open so I wanted to come and witness what is inside. I am just curious, a wander-esse you know?'*

Wanderment Exercise #

Date: 13 of December 2021
Location: Terazije towards Carigradska street, Belgrade
Duration: 1h
Props: smartphone

Are you hungry? Yes.
I accepted the invitation for dinner.

Exiting the apartment, I decided not to take the regular fast route towards hers home, intending to wander a bit – deliberately. It had snowed so beautifully the day before and I wished to witness that time in the city before the show would melt and things go back to the way they were. At the crossroad, I choose the other path and had a thought *'nothing new there'*, and just like that on my left the view towards a new world opened. Those doors were open, and that whole wide world inside of it as well.

I stepped inside carefully looking at the giant pink *fuckpolitics* graffiti and beneath it a bathtub and bags of construction leftovers. What a treat already for my sore mind. I walked towards the next open door and thought *'Wooow, how big is this space inside; I wonder if I could go through the whole block?'* I stepped inside into the snow, a man with a dog walked by me, entered one of the entrance doors inside the yard. The sight was familiar – similar to a courtyard in Zemun, but also to that one in Ljubljana, and also like the one... I started turning around and all the walls were covered with graffiti traces – inscriptions of different entities, groups, subgroups, textures, ideologies. The inner walls were visually and metaphorically shouting, screaming with layered and dense demands, statements and inscriptions of various kinds. Like an open-air museum of subcultural voicing. I walked further, and then the borders came: inner borders, fences, divisions inside the block, and new graffities on the other side, again shouting, demanding. Actually it all felt as a forum, an arena, a place to state your piece of mind. I hoped there was a path behind the trafostation house inside the yard, but all I could do was go around it and see it becoming yet another place taken over by graffiti. As if this courtyard was the moon and all those 'wanderers (flâneurs)' like myself being provoked by it curiously came in and then left traces of their endeavor, marking territory. Still, it was not flâneurs leaving traces, it was territory markings of the locals, sending out the message who is who inside that small but big system as it felt.

'I only left my footsteps in the snow', I thought. Exited and taking the last photo with my phone, my eyes rolled up seeing the red lights of the security

camera. I felt busted. I felt insecure about my endeavor and my action. I thought to myself: *'What are you doing? Why do you need this, why do you have to know, why do you have to take pictures, why do you need this, is it worth it, someone can go after you.'* The words, opinions others would say to me for my actions and desire for discovering and wandering echoed in me. The wonderment was over, the excitement of discovery was over. Is there anything to discover that these cameras don't know yet, is there some corner to go where your traces are the first ones in snow?

I felt busted that night but still, streets are there on google maps street view, google cars passed through them and who asked if I/we wanted this to be traced. Should I start google street wa(o)nderments?

After a wanderment act, the presence of a street is never perceived the same way. Now, I see, I feel through the building walls that take me to that inner shouting courtyard. I remember the very first time of my life stepping into this street; it felt like a breeze behind the formal side of the parliament building. Little and intimate.

'Cities are like onions, layered, by removing each layer of them we might start to cry for so many different reasons.'

Wanderment Inscribing experience #

Date: 28 of October 2021
Location: Belgrade, Pajsijeva street
Duration: 1h
Props: Chalk

The need to inscribe came as a result of regular wanderments in a close radius of where I currently live. The habit consists of me taking time to go through this area in search of something new, exploring corners, passing all the streets in a new way – like walking on the other side of the street, looking up, or looking into the front facades etc.

Almost two years ago, I encountered this street in a new way looking at it from across the road, noticing differently the qualities given to it by its geographical position. This street is narrow and steep; from where I was looking at it, it only goes up. Walking through, it feels like being in a canyon. It feels domestic due to the sound of clinking of dishes from the inside of the apartments. It has small balconies facing each other and, by my calculation, a quite surprising number of residents. It feels quite intimate, yet abandoned. Looking at it from that point and place, I saw the street as a blank paper rolling in front of those apartments looking upon it. I felt the urge to write on it – to treat it as such.

During those days, I was repeating the lyrics of the poem *"No te Rindas"* (engl. *'Do not give up'*) by Mario Benedetti wandering around. I wanted to write those specific lyrics there, on that street paper. It seemed appropriate to use the street to leave such writing as a message, as a gift to all those who wander in life.

We were planning to visit an exhibition near my apartment in a ruined hotel building, but it was closed – we had time left and started walking. I remembered that street and asked him to join me in an inscribing journey. I bought the chalk on the way and entered the street noticing it has a brand-new asphalt on it, ready and perfected for writing. So I started inscribing. With each new line I wrote, I thought of giving up as my back was hurting while writing in the steep street.

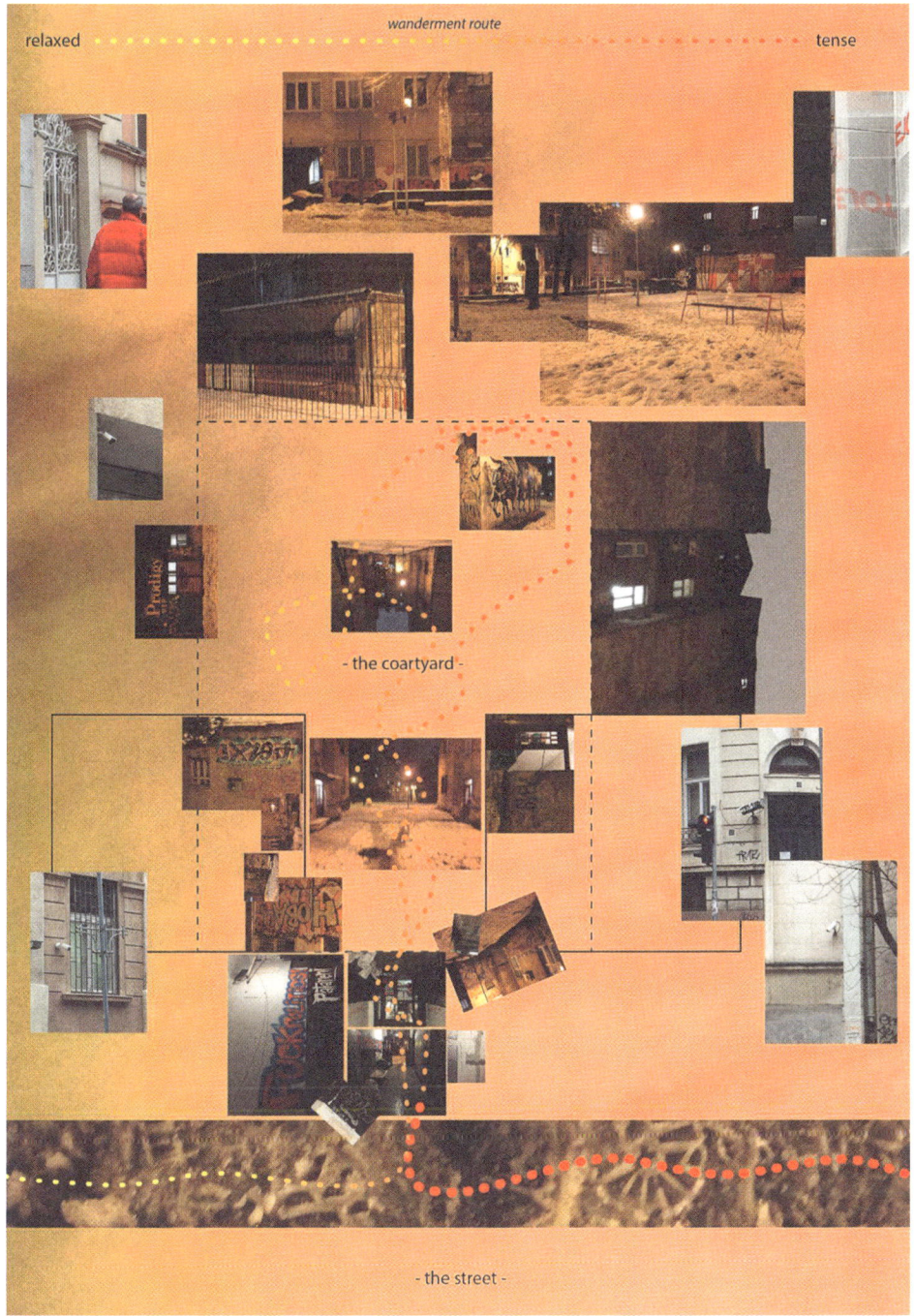

Inner courtyard photo collage map: birds view

People passed by; man, women, father with daughter, neighbors were sneaking by, looking at the act of inscribing. No one asked a thing, only a lady passing by said what I was doing was beautiful. A man stopped and read a few lines. Kids turned around. He said *'I hope neighbors don't report us.'* I looked at the cameras in front of the residential entrances facing me while inscribing. I felt dizzy and my legs started to shake. *'The letters become longer and bigger'*, he said. I stopped in the middle of the street, in the middle point of the poem.

The next day I came back to the scene; this time from the top, facing a downward direction. It seemed like someone had washed the whole street. Only when coming closer, I could see that the letters were still there but slightly washed away by passing cars. I wondered *'what do they look like from above – the apartments?'*

On the third day, when I visited again, the letters had disappeared. The graffiti on the side walls were still there.

NOTES IN CLOSING

These wanderings were the result of the particular lived experience of the wandering women involved in the given moment of writing, as a practice of participatory knowing and document of experiential learning. The difference among the accounts amounts to the specificity of partial perspectives in conversation that happens inevitably within a collective of researchers and asks the question how the differences can be honed in on when engaged in collaborative work. The three exercises offer three distinct perspectives spoken from the body, (per-)forming knowledge spaces from corporeal involvement in its immediate surroundings. They follow the principles of data feminism (challenging power, elevating emotion and embodiment, rethinking binaries and hierarchies, embracing pluralism, considering context, making labor visible) in conversation with feminist new materialisms, applied to the practice of walking in lived public spaces inhabited by human and more than human agents and experiences. As such, they represent a deeply somatic application of data feminist research into the act of flânerie and open the question of broadening the space of perspectival and participatory knowing together with creating more space for them within research frameworks.

Photo collage of Pajsijeva street top-down-top directions

4th Part

Situated Experiences while Walking

Dorothea Hamilton

2,54 cm away from Flying – Or: Walking in the Skies as a Feminist

My heart is racing, my legs are shaking. Underneath me, there is one inch then nothing. 40 meters of nothingness. I am sitting on a one-inch-line that is 2,54 centimeters wide but 140-meter-long. As I sit with one leg on the line and the other one hanging next to it, I feel the tension in my body and the slackline's tension under my tailbone. My mind is blank. All I know is that I want to walk on this line, to walk in the skies as I have done before. I remember the feeling of putting one foot in front of the other and balancing over the valley beneath me. I remember the shaking of the line, the feeling of control and losing it. I recall the feeling of the soft sway of the tensioned line underneath my feet. They say it is 17 kilonewton, but really, I have no idea what that number means. To me, it means nothing. It is just me sitting on a line, scared to death to stand up and walk.

Walking feels like heaven. But first, I will have to stand up – that is all I remember. Again, I check my gear. My harness is tight and the leash that will save me from dying is attached to the harness and the line. Both will prevent me from falling 40 m to the ground. "Nothing will happen, you are fine", I hear myself saying. "You are safe, this will hold you. You are alright", repeats my brain with a calming voice. I lift my second leg on the line, the first step to stand up. My abdominals contract. "Now stand up!" I hear the voice of an inner coach with little patience. My heartbeat rises as if morsing me 'YOU WILL DIE'. "Oh come on", says the coach to the morsing heart. "Why am I doing this?", pops up into my brain. I take my leg down again. "Oh come on", says the coach's voice somewhat annoyed, "you are so privileged, you have come all the way here, you have no kids today, no work, it's just you on this line and you will walk!" I remember my friend saying: "Smile and enjoy your surroundings." I try. I see the treetops underneath. I watch a squirrel on the ground and some birds swirling around me. Still, it is hard to enjoy when you are scared to death. The view is stunning, but my fear is worse.

As I watch a bird flying beneath me, I remember the three hours it took to pull the line from one tree to another and tie it to the trees. I also remember the many walks through a wet forest to find a suitable spot. The climbing of many trees, the use of a 'ranger', a device used to measure the length. The many discussions about whether the ratio between the length and the height was still safe. The calculations, the scratches from thorns and trees as if taking their tribute for this moment. A new voice turns up: "Who am I to measure this magical space of a forest and reduce it to numbers instead of enjoying the innumerable sensory impressions?" Maybe the man who passed by the other day was right when he said: "You are destroying our forest". But are we really? Who did he refer to when he said 'our' forest? Are we not just another animal sitting on this line trying to co-exist in this world we are sharing with other beings? My arms are still up, my shoulders are hurting, a pigeon is flying by.

I now remember the hours it took to tighten the line after finding this spot above this valley. The specialized equipment demanded so much of my attention – and that had excluded me so long from being part of the crew. Then, the strength of at least three strong humans – generally men – to tighten the pulley system. I also remember the hours walking through the misty forest at dawn to get here. The brisk air, the cold feet and I think of all the other things I could have done with the day. But here I am, here, just for this one moment. "Why did I come? Why put so much effort, time, and gear just to sit here and be scared?", my fearful self asks. "Because you can and because it's great", answers the inner coach. "No is not an option", I answer in my mind. "It's not cool to be scared,

I hate highlining!", answers the scared heartbeat. A moment of silence, inside and out. Only the sound of moving leaves and the unregular beat of my heart. I try to concentrate on my surroundings. The birds I am closer to than normally, the unusual view. In vain. "Perhaps I should go back", crosses my mind. Back, that means pulling myself to the anchor point using all my muscles. I would arrive sweating and red-faced and would greet the others. "No, you will not", answers the merciless inner self, "you will at least try to stand up." "But why?", I ask scaredly. "Because you are the quota woman!", answers the self with no mercy. "Really, I don't need this. Maybe I should make some muffins or do yoga to feel good, or something else I learned women do to feel good." I am the only woman in the group – as usual in German highlining. Of course, it would be ok to not try, that is the privilege of being a woman. Nobody expects me to perform, fear is accepted for persons of my gender. But overcoming fear is something I learn in this practice. "No way I will do what they expect", I answer myself and put my leg back on the line. I remember all those women who say: "Maybe next time I will try." Dedication enters my body. I remember a breathing technique. Inhale twice, exhale once: In-in-out. In-in-out. I raise my arms and feel the balance. I feel the others observing me as body on the line. "Now!", says the inner coach. "Now you show them that women..." – "That woman what?", answers my body again. I drop my leg down again and think about this group that we are. 5–10 men and me. It took a year until they joined me in their Telegram-messenger group. They have their ways of communicating: This includes the naming of all the technical devices. The knowledge that shows that you are part of the highliners – or that excludes those who do not know the name of every specialized object that enables us to be up here. It excludes those who call the line a "slackline" and not a "webbing". Or those who do not know how much stretch each webbing has. Besides learning their vocabulary I also had to learn their codes: The way they show appreciation, the way to know who is accepted and who is not, the way they talk about their success when they come down from the line, the way they (do not) address feelings and imperfections. All year long, I felt I had to learn a new language. No one urged me to, of course not, but without that, I would have felt excluded, like all the other women who had participated a few times and then did not return. Perhaps this answers in part why there are so few women. And of course, there is a physical disadvantage that matters especially in the beginning. But here I am, after so much hardship. "Enjoy!", urges the inner coach. Instead, I think about my outfit and the patriarchal conducts I am confronted with. They say: "May I help you?"; "Be careful, don't fall!" – and prevent me from learning through these helping gestures. I get mad about having to even think about what clothes I wear – or do any of the men think about that? When I ask them why there are so few women on the line, they answer: "I don't know, they probably don't like it", or: "We are not excluding anybody here", or: "Women are just not so interested in technical things", or: "The other day Sara came, too", or: "Why are you asking me, do you think I am sexist?" I close my eyes for a second, remembering all these moments. Sometimes I feel I think too much about gender when I am on the line, but I also feel somewhat lonely because I am the only woman in the area with that level of experience. I feel that it is no coincidence that it is that way. I feel that highlining makes hidden structures visible.

I feel the line under my tailbone again. I imagine my daughter watching. I want to be that mother who tried to walk. Even if she fell. I want her to hear the others say: "Look, your mom is walking… look, she stood up again!" And I imagine her answering distractedly: "Yeah, I know, why shouldn't she?" I put my leg on the line. At this moment, I am searching for role models in my head. Women who stood up once more than they had fallen. Mothers who, besides taking care of their children's needs, are brave enough to try things they are scared of, who do not back up against comfortable role models but challenge them, even if it means crossing their limits. Amazons on lines. Worrioresses in the air who prove to their children that being a woman does not mean being weak or conforming with existing norms. "When do women unlearn to be beings who are scared and have the strength to overcome this fear? When can we stop asking if we are too female or not female enough? When do we start to just do what we want instead of thinking about how we are seen?" My legs are now both on the line. I focus my sight on a branch on the other side of the valley. I take a deep breath. The line is shaking. This time, I do not care. "Now!", says the coach. I push my legs into the shaking line. I am standing! I am alive. My arms are wide open and tense as if I could hold on to an imaginary rope. Carefully, I put one foot in front of the other. I just took my first step, a spark of joy in my head. My arms balance the moving line and the shaking of my legs. Another step. My eyes clamp to the branch on the other side. "You are walking in the skies!", I tell myself, "Breathe." My heart is racing. "Breathe." My legs are shaking. I try to prevent them from moving against my will but they do not stop, I have to live my fear. I take the next step. "Two, three", I count as I walk. The line starts to shake and my upper body leans to the right side, it feels like I will fall. "Four, five." A movement of my arms to the left. "Don't fall! Six, seven." Everything else becomes inexistent. Everything but the line and me. All that exists at this moment is the flow of my body and the concentration and the cold air. I forget the men sitting down on the ground watching. "Eight, nine." I feel my arms aching. "Keep going", the inner coach reminds me. "Ten, eleven." I start to sweat. "Twelve." My legs are shaking. I am still walking in the skies, but I feel that I will fall soon. I am scared of dying. "Thirteen." A movement to the right; I try to focus on breathing. My heart is racing. "You – fourteen – can – fifteen – do – sixteen – this – seventeen." I am focusing on the other side. I am focusing, all the rest of existence becomes a blur. "Eighteen." I long to cross this line. "Nineteen." I know I will not. "Twenty." A short celebration. "Keep going!" For a moment, I feel comfortable, my legs are shaking less. The line is shaking less. "Twenty-one – Don't give up – twenty-two." I feel my strength is leaving me. I feel the sweat on my forehead and my back, my contracting muscles, and the moving line under my feet. "Twenty-three, twenty-four." I want to vomit. I move my arms with a brisk movement to the right. "Twenty-five." I lose balance, I cannot hold myself any longer. I fall.

    For a moment, I remember nothing. Then I find myself hanging under the line, attached to the leash. I just walked twenty-five steps through the skies. I am alive. A moment of rejoicing. The next moment: "Why didn't I manage to walk further?" "Great!", I congratulate myself on the other hand. I hear the men cheering. A moment of rest. Then I have to get back on the line. I climb the leash, I feel the rope cutting into my legs, I feel the disadvantage of having to pull more weight with fewer muscles with that female body that I have. This is the moment when it is easier if you have less body fat, but yes, it is possible with my body, too. I pull myself up, swing my leg around the line, I am sitting again. I am exhausted. I want to get to the other side. I will have to try again. "Stand up once more than you fall", I tell myself. My heart is racing, my legs are shaking. I will try again, try to walk through the skies. And sometimes I wish I could motivate more women to do so.

EPILOGUE

The text above was written seven months ago. Many leash falls have happened. Now I am sitting next to a line that is 400 m long in southern Spain. Two other women are present, watching the other woman on the line. She is coming back. I am waiting for my turn on that line. I have never walked on a line that long, that high. But I feel comfortable about the idea. No need to prove anything to anyone, I just want to enjoy the moment. Seeing other women walk, fall, and get up again gives me a feeling of comfort, even though I know that it does not matter if you are male or female on the line. Here, for the first time, I see several women walking on long lines – and yes, it makes a difference. Why, I do not know.

Now, it is my turn. Here I am, 3000 km away from home, obligations, and kids. I have taken the time to come all the way here for walking this line during this little highline gathering close to Granada. But really, the geography does not matter much. It could be anywhere. My life with its hustles, obligations, fixed dates and crowded space is far away. I see the steep hills covered with bushes and the snow-covered mountain Sierra Nevada behind them. I feel chilled by the morning mist although the sun rays are warming my skin. I look at my clothes and imagine what I look like. I have been sleeping in tents and cars for the last few weeks. According to urban standards I am dirty and probably carry an unpleasant smell. I have not seen myself in the mirror since I left. But I feel strong surrounded by the slope and harsh nature and the other females in this environment. I look at them, dirty as I am, and I think: "I am a warrior-esse." And then my eyes fall on the small but strong olive tree the long line is attached to. It is impressive how such a small creature can hold such an absurd weight. I check if the attached line is safe, I fasten the safety knot of the leash, one of the women double checks it, I grab the line, move away from the ground to gain safety. Yes, it is as paradoxical as it seems – the further the ground is away the safer it gets.

"Go for it!", I hear one of the women say and I smile as I sway myself on the line with that movement I have done so many times. I sit up, feel their gaze on me but my thoughts are clear. I take a deep breath. I put my foot on the line. I cannot even see where the line is attached on the other side, that is how far it is away. I concentrate on the next marker on the line. I stand up. "This line feels different", comes into my mind. It's movements are very slow; it almost feels like I have to communicate with this line. "She feels like an old lady", I had heard someone say about it. I take one step. I move my arms too much. I fall. I pull myself up again, sit straight. I am getting used to this particular movement. I breathe. In-In-Out. I stand up again. I breathe. I feel comfortable. I forget the height. I concentrate on my focus point. I take another step, my shoulders are soft, there is no fear. No fear of falling. No fear of not performing. Just me, walking on the line. "Three, four, five, six, seven, eight." – "Why am I still counting steps?", I ask myself with no need to answer. "Nine, ten, eleven." It is just the way I walk. I try to focus and relax my body. "Twelve, thirteen, fourteen, fifteen." I see my surrounding. Birds flying way below me, another highline about 100 m below. The mountains, the hills, the sky. While I am walking, I feel gratitude for all the circumstances that have made this absurdity possible. "Sixteen, seventeen, eighteen, nineteen, twenty, twenty-one." I remember a friend saying: "To me, the most important thing is to walk relaxed." I smile as I remember my hometown and the men I have been on the line with so many times. "Twenty-two, twenty-three, twenty-four – walk relaxed – twenty-five, twenty-six." I wish they could see me, not to show off but to share this moment. "Twenty-seven, twenty-eight." While I walk and count, I feel grateful for everyone who has made this possible. "Twenty-nine, thirty." I hear the girls cheering at the anchor point. "Thirty-one, thirty-two, thirty-three, thirty-four, thirty-five, thirty-six." I fall. "That's ok." I watch the line below me. I am 150 meters off the ground and probably 40 meters from the anchor. I am all by myself. And I am not. I hear the women cheering, I know it is important for them to see me cross this line – no matter how many times I fall. "Watching you was an inspiration", a young woman says later, as even here, only a few women are crossing to the other side. "Stand up once more then you fall." That is my lesson from highlining. I stand up. I take one step. Another. And another. I am walking in the skies. I am the sky. I smile.

So why do I call highlining a feminist practice? To me, the missing women in this sport unveil much of the societal structures of who we learn to be as women in a patriarchal society. We learn to rather not try than to fall, to rather observe than fail to try. We learn to have technical issues resolved by men. We learn that it is ok not to push our limits. To become part of a male-dominated field we have to learn that language and their codes. We are many times, intentionally or unintentionally, excluded. And, of course, we have to fight for the time on the line as most of the invisible care work is done by us. Also, there is an actual constant threat of sexual assault. But if women see women walking on a line, this will – hopefully – crumble away little by little. I wish for my kids to see more women who stood up despite their fear.

Close-ups: Anton Glaap from below
Michael Streuber

Susanne Nemmerz
Long-Distance Hiking – Arriving. Lingering. Walking on.[1]

[1] This is a slightly adapted translation of the already published text: *Weit Wandern – Ankommen/Verweilen/Weitergehen. Eine Raumerfahrung in der Bewegung* [*Walking far – arriving/pausing/moving on: A spatial experience in motion*]. In J. Bilstein & H. Peskoller (Eds.), Erfahrung – Erfahrungen. Wiesbaden: VS, 285–294

AN EXPERIENCE OF SPACE IN MOVEMENT

We move about in environments that we perceive with our senses. We smell, see, taste, touch, and hear – we sense by means of our bodies. These sensory impressions influence what we feel – that is, our sensory immersion in space. We perceive these individual impressions consciously or unconsciously. All of our spatial perceptions and experiences are inextricably linked with the experience of our own lived body: "We live in spaces and we think spatially."[2] Spaces are experienced and are constituted by boundaries that separate the inside from the outside.

"Every human being is intimately involved in its environment, moves in the flow of actions through time and space, is influenced by its environment, and influences this environment her*himself. Both effect, disturb, complement, or adapt to one another."[3]

Space is experienced individually, and this perception of space is a process that is not the same for everyone.[4] Analyzing the formation of space requires that we include the perspective of human beings within their networks of relations as well as their corporal and sensory abilities.

We rarely attempt to understand how we as corporal beings create spaces.[5] In the following, I draw on my long-distance hiking experiences in the Pyrenees to illuminate the interrelations between humans and space and make them accessible. Long-distance hiking is a mode of being on the move in a simple, archaic way, carrying only the bare necessities in a backpack. It is a slow process of 'being on the way' intensely experiencing space and time. In this text, I will trace what the hiker does when looking for and finding a campsite after a day of hiking in the mountains, when setting up his*her bivouac, spending the night there, dismantling it in the morning, and continuing to hike until the end of the next day, at which point they s*he looks for a campsite again, thus continuing another cycle.

This arriving, lingering, walking on, moving from one place to the next, and bivouacking in a place is the focus of my interest. The decisive experience that I have when hiking long-distance is that spaces in and of themselves are not simply there. Spaces are relational. They emerge through my activity and can also disappear through a shift in activity and sensory attention.[6] Yet they remain existent in my imagination. In my research, I assume a relational conception of space in which spaces are derived from positional relationships and are thus created in situated constellations of materialities, sensory perceptions, and imaginations/memories of humans.

[2] Becker, G., Bilstein, J., & Liebau, E. (Eds.). (1997). *Räume bilden: Studien zur pädagogischen Topologie und Topographie* [*Shaping spaces: Studies on pedagogical topology and topography*]. Seelze-Velber: Kallmeyersche Verlagsbuchhandlung, p. 9

[3] Frers, L. (2006). *Einhüllende Materialitäten: Eine Phänomenologie des Wahrnehmens und Handelns an Bahnhöfen und Fährterminals* [*Enveloping materialities: A phenomenology of perception and action at train stations and ferry terminals*]. Bielefeld: transcript Verlag, p. 39

[4] Löw, M. (2001). *Raumsoziologie* [*Sociology of space*]. Frankfurt am Main: Suhrkamp Verlag, p. 197

[5] ibid., p. 161

[6] Schroer, M. (2006). *Räume, Orte, Grenzen: Auf dem Weg zu einer Soziologie des Raums* [*Spaces, places, boundaries: Towards a sociology of space*]. Frankfurt am Main: Suhrkamp, p. 174

ARRIVING

Bivouacking[7] presupposes a place to set up the bivouac. While hiking [far away from the amenities of human settlements], one needs to find a place to spend the night outdoors. Mountains have their own spatial and material patterns; they have been created over spans of time unperceivable for humans and exist in their own temporality. They are a heterogeneous, diverse natural environment that features a great variety of forms and shapes no matter how small the area.

In the mountains, no place was designed to my vision of it. There are no given domestic arrangements. In a sense, I am required to reinvent the place where I want to settle for the night and place myself amidst the given material surrounding and life.

[7] Here, bivouacking refers to setting up a campsite in the mountains for the duration of one night

Vorblick – Foresight

It takes more than one's simple spatial presence to create a bivouac in a place. Using and appropriating a given situation for a specific purpose requires certain cultural practices and a corresponding habitus.[8]

My expectations of what a place to stay should look like and my intentions are closely related to my previous experiences. If I had been walking in strong wind all day, my perception will likely be geared towards finding a place that is [shielded from wind and] as calm as possible. My perceptions and actions will be tied to this expectation.

Once I arrive at my destination for the day, my horizon narrows from "the vastness of the landscape" to "a possible place to spend the night that spans a few square meters." The possible overnight accommodation is small compared to the vastness of the landscape. This small area is investigated with an open eye and considered in all its differences in search of a comfortable place to stay for the night.

As I refocus my attention, niches, angles, options to lean up against, areas for lying down, and warmth take shape; as I do so, my perceptions and actions broaden the world. Each shift in my focus of attention gives rise to a specific space that presents itself to me as a perceiving and acting agent.[9]

The environment, the things that are present, the other person with whom I am hiking, and I, all this together produces what happens in this place. In this process, I intertwine myself with those others. The connections between the things, that which is given in the situation, and my own corporeality are of decisive importance for the emerging spatial situation.[10]

8 ibid., p. 97

9 Frers, 2007, p. 53

10 ibid., p. 37

Biwak – Bivouac

In the continuous interplay of how I relate to the world with my senses and through my actions, my perceptions and actions emerge. In my perceptions and actions, I interact with my surroundings. In doing so, I interrelate and combine various elements of action. My perceptions are attuned to acts of movement and communication that can only be grasped relationally.

HOW DO I PERCEIVE?

What are the conditions in my environment? How do I feel? Do my impressions meet my expectations? Is it windy or not? At what are my actions directed? Initially, scanning the ground? Which conditions might be important for setting camp? Will the rock roll away if I lean my backpack up against it? Is the spot level or does it slope to one side? Do I have to watch my steps? Is the path from my tent entrance to the cooking area bumpy? Does the rock have sharp edges? Is it comfortable to sit on?
How am I moving about? Are my movements slow or fast? How much attention am I giving the other person? How much attention is that person demanding? Will the sun quickly disappear behind the mountain, or will my damp hiking clothes still be able to dry a little when I lay them out on a rock? The temperature will definitely change significantly. The wind can affect my hearing. Changes in the wind can alter the odorous landscape. Moisture can feel clammy.[11]

All of these perceptions are present when I set up the campsite. They point to options and constraints and shape my impressions of the place and my feelings about it. These impressions are related to my own corporal condition. Depending on the mood that I am in, I will perceive my impressions with greater or lesser intensity and my perceptions and actions will change.[12]

Completing the various activities takes time. And the length of time I need, say, to fetch drinking water will influence my experience of this place.

[11] Frers, 2007, p. 25

[12] ibid., p. 66

LINGERING

When setting the campsite, not only the things that I have brought along in my backpack are of relevance but also the affordances of my surrounding.[13] How this campsite will take shape depends on the natural conditions – "where there is no river, it cannot be included in the constitution of space" (ibid.). It will also depend on what I have experienced before. A river that I may have had to cross will shape my subsequent spatial practices.

[13] Löw, 2001, p. 191

My bodily possibilities and necessities, my habitus, as well as the corporality of both things and humans will influence the creation of the bivouac.

Setting up a campsite involves placing things: my tent, hiking sticks, cookware, clothing, backpack, and so on. This placement is an act of negotiation and fitting the things brought along into what is already there.

WHAT DO I FEEL?

Once I have set everything up, I soon feel a sense of well-being. I know that this sensation has something to do with me, with the things, with the other human being, with everything encountered and that has happened in this place. I can sense it with my body. Sensing with my lived body, I distinguish between the realms of the inside and the outside.

In between, there is something that exists in my imagination. It was created in the course of my actions in this place without adhering to a given materiality. Yet, it has a shape, a *gestalt*.[14] It is an inherently invisible construct, an ensemble that I have formed into a single element through my perception, imagination, and memory. Only that which is related to one another, which has formed into an inside and outside, is existent for me.[15] In my imagination, what has formed between me and my surroundings can be perceived materially as a space. I can perceive the inclusive and exclusive character of this space with my senses.[16] In this process of creating a materially perceptible space, I cannot describe the "material" as something concrete or measure it precisely. I know that there is something subtle about the experience that makes it difficult to grasp or understand how it actually emerges. Yet the notion of having created a materially perceptible space allows me to put this experience into words.[17] The environment affects me, does something to me, while I likewise create the environment through my actions. The materially perceptible space is produced from both the outside and the inside. It protrudes into both and is also between the two.

I have outlined the felt boundary between me and my surroundings in a sketch of the campsite. I am able to draw this boundary in my sketch, but looking for it in the terrain would be to no avail. This boundary corresponds with the [felt] need for inclusion and exclusion. Transgressing it makes its existence feel even more real. Once established, this imaginary line cannot be erased.[18]

14
Löw, 2001, p. 191

15
ibid., p. 159

16
ibid., p. 204

17
At this point, I would like to refer to Lars Frers' study *Einhüllende Materialitäten* (2007); Enveloping Materialities. This study applies video analysis and ethnographic observation to explore the material reality of the everyday world at train stations and ferry terminals as experienced through the senses. Drawing on phenomenological foundations, Frers conceives of the concept of envelopment to gain a grasp of the emergence of materially perceptible space.

18
Kamper, D. (1998). *Von Wegen* [*Of paths*]. München: Wilhelm Fink Verlag, p. 14

Map of camp site

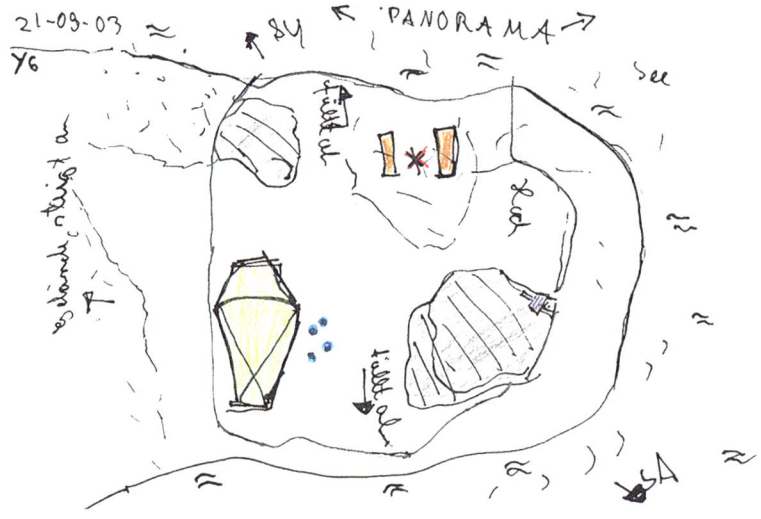

This sketch shows the position of things: the tent, the cooking area, the sitting areas, the walking sticks.

> I tried to grasp the situation at the site in the way that the situation spoke to me physically.
>
> My drawing displays the position of things
>
> such as the tent
>
> in relation to the positions of other things

such as the hiking sticks or the cooking area and in their relative position to the natural conditions and the topography. It depicts the way that these relations appeared to me. The sketch contains the date, and arrows inform of the cardinal points of the compass.

I have also included the line of the felt boundary mentioned above. This sketch attempts to capture my individual sense of space. It emerged from my own feeling for the situation in this place. Someone else would experience the situation in this place differently.

The impressions that contribute to the constitution of this space come from all directions, sometimes strongly and sometimes more subtly. This materially perceptible space is produced in the encounter with concrete spatial, social, and material constellations and features specific properties accordingly, such as a certain size and shape. This created space guards against certain perceptions ensures that I do not focus my attention on certain impressions. This is how I protect myself from excitement and distraction.[20] In particular, the "materialization of space" can conceal those aspects that I perceive as disruptive or risky. The materially perceptible space regulates the range of perception and thus also the range of action.[21] It enables me to pursue my goals-for instance, to eat and sleep-as undisturbed as possible in one place. It establishes affiliations and regulates access. Within this boundary, I can gain a sense of having an overview[, of being in control].

The bivouac offers me a retreat and makes it easier for me to relax.[22] It creates a sense of security. For the duration of one night, the bivouac becomes a place of orientation to which everything in the area is related. It allows me to organize a transition between the familiar and the unfamiliar, the known and the unknown. Among the familiar are the way back and the things that I carry with me. The familiar includes the procedures of setting up and dismantling the tent, of packing, and unpacking the backpack. As long as I can engage in these familiar actions, they provide me with a sense of security and stability. Here, the felt boundary establishes a relationship between the proximate and the distant. This opportunity to retreat enables me to see the foreign still ahead of me as an enrichment. This investment in a dividing line, which defines an inside and outside, provides relief and security, creates clarity, stability, and promises the ability to keep an overview of [and control over] a [potentially] confusing world.[23]

[19] Frers, 2007, p. 54

[20] ibid., p. 55

[21] ibid., p. 82

[22] Peskoller, H. (2007). Biwak. In C. Wulf & J. Zirfass (Eds.), *Muße. Paragrana, 16*(1). Berlin: Akademie Verlag, 113–125

[23] Schroer, 2006, p. 69

WALKING ON

The experience of space that I am describing here is a fundamental experience of perceiving and sensing. It is inherently in motion and transitory. Bivouacking implies arriving, lingering, and walking on. Before I settle in, I know that I intend to walk on, that I intend to leave again. Ahead is a[nother] new environment waiting to be experienced.

Departing in the morning confronts me with abandoning what has now become familiar to me for a yet unknown future. The space that I have created by the activities I have engaged in begins to dwindle as my activities cease in this place. [Yet] my memory merges the bivouac and the place into a single element of remembrance. In my imagination, this bivouac continues to exist.[24] My impact on this place only has a short life, as wind and water along with the weather and the workings of nature will erase it again.

[24] Löw, 2001, p. 199

The abandoned bivouac site is now behind me and the next one lies ahead of me. I am moving forward, and at the beginning of the hike, I feel at home, connected to the previous campsite. I perceive myself in relation to the previous site and what I am leaving behind at an ever-greater distance. What I am feeling is directed backward as opposed to my walking forward. I am entangled in a relation. I need this relation with the abandoned site to be able to think of myself in reference to a [place that is] home.

IN THE REALM OF THE IN-BETWEEN

Hiking constitutes a space that differs from one bivouac site to the next. There is a bivouac of origin and a bivouac of arrival. In between there is hiking. As one moves on, the bivouac of arrival becomes a bivouac of origin. The emerging space-in-between is made up of elements of both and is thus also something new.[25]

When hiking long distances, I proceed to a different geographical location yet maintain an intense bond with the previous campsite. The places that I have experienced are connected in my imagination. New interrelations are created that span through time and space. As the hike unfolds, more and more campsites are added. It is a 'being on the way' that is embedded in the vastness. A space of movement that is constituted and reconstituted over and over again through movement.

[25] Schroer, 2006, p. 211

FROM PLACE TO PLACE

Long-distance hiking entails a constant change in perception and thus in how one positions oneself in the world. In this 'being on the way,' perceiving and doing are continuously realigned. My relation to the environment changes. With the decision to move on comes not only a change in attitude but invariably also a realignment of perception and action. The act of being outside the bivouac site is different from that of being within. Once I leave the site behind, a differentiated world opens up – a world full of options that I have yet to grasp. The realm of possibilities that unfolds before me is vast. I must reorganize my mode of perception and action for the purpose of walking on. This requires reorienting myself and choosing between a variety of possible lines of action.

It is a process of sensibilization within my field of perception. I can grasp my own situatedness in the world and, on this foundation, act in the world based on my decisions and orientations.

As I go from place to place, I make comparisons and my view is sharpened for the details of a place and its peculiarities. I traverse distinct environments. I bring eating habits and objects with me and use them in a new world of which I am now part. I have experiences, and they provide certainty, and more experiences are awaiting me, and this is too is a certainty. I practice the act of setting up camp. As I repeatedly transition through these passages and different places, I engage in efforts to insert myself and adapt.[26] This yields sensory specialization and diversification.

[26] Frers, 2007, p. 72

Space becomes perceptible to me, and thus existent, by me relating the materiality of things, humans, and natural conditions, my memory, my habitus, my corporal possibilities, and necessities to one another. This perception of space is still there in my memory. I have stored these relations.

Such experiences of space are acts of practicing spatial awareness. They represent instances of learning to think in relations. For an anthropology of space, the question of relational space conceptions is central – especially through the reference to the experience of the body in motion. The long-distance hikes in the Pyrenees illuminate the relation of material conditions and bodies-in-movement as relational becoming.

Abdruck – Impression

Regula Pöhl & Daniela Villiger / Zündwerk
Every Wednesday. Action 05–20

the same way
the same route

Distance 16.4 km
Duration 4h 15 min
Ascent 63 m
Descent 171 m
Highest point 551 m
Lowest point 411 m

"starting from your own home
walking in the opposite direction
approaching each other
up to the point of encounter"

a project by Daniela Villiger, Wetzikon 47°19'15 "N 8°47'36" E
and Regula Pöhl, Rapperswil 47°13'43 "N 8°49'54" E

How does it feel to walk toward each other on a regular basis?
This question was the starting point of our project, Action 05–20.

In our collaboration, we always approach each other in a figurative sense and meet wherever there is resonance. In this project, our focus is on the lived and embodied experience of approaching each other. By repeating it again and again, we are creating an imaginary drawing in the space. In this sense, our working principle of engaging in dialogue with a counterpart is realized within (a) material space/a landscape.

Every wednesday...

"I close my apartment door, go down the stairwell, and cross the neighborhood. My attention is slowly dissolving from everyday life to the crunching of the stones under my feet. My steps are getting faster. The wide plain of meadows and fields is pulling my thoughts into the distance. The landscape is changing slowly, a kind of standstill; words are circling above my head in different constellations. I walk along the familiar path half consciously.

In the industrial area, a pedestrian crossing interrupts my flow of movement. My thoughts are as disorganized as the random ensembles of buildings. Only by the forest, my senses calm down. The noise from the outside world is swallowed and my own steps are audible. Upright stand the trees, and upright becomes my walk. Eyes and mind are clear and alert, in the very moment.

I know the way only into one direction. Southwards. Sometimes the landscape moves past me and I feel like sitting on a train. Sometimes the space seems to be non-existent and I can no longer remember the crossing I just passed. And sometimes I struggle with every step and wish that you will approach me very soon. Then, suddenly, you appear. Every time, it is a little bit unexpected. Absorbed in thoughts, the moment of encounter suddenly becomes real. We face each other. The tension eases. Relaxation. Together we deviate from the predetermined path and exchange our thoughts, our impressions of the path. At our meeting point, time stands still. We say good bye. Till next week. And I will go to the next best bus or train station and dive back into my everyday life."

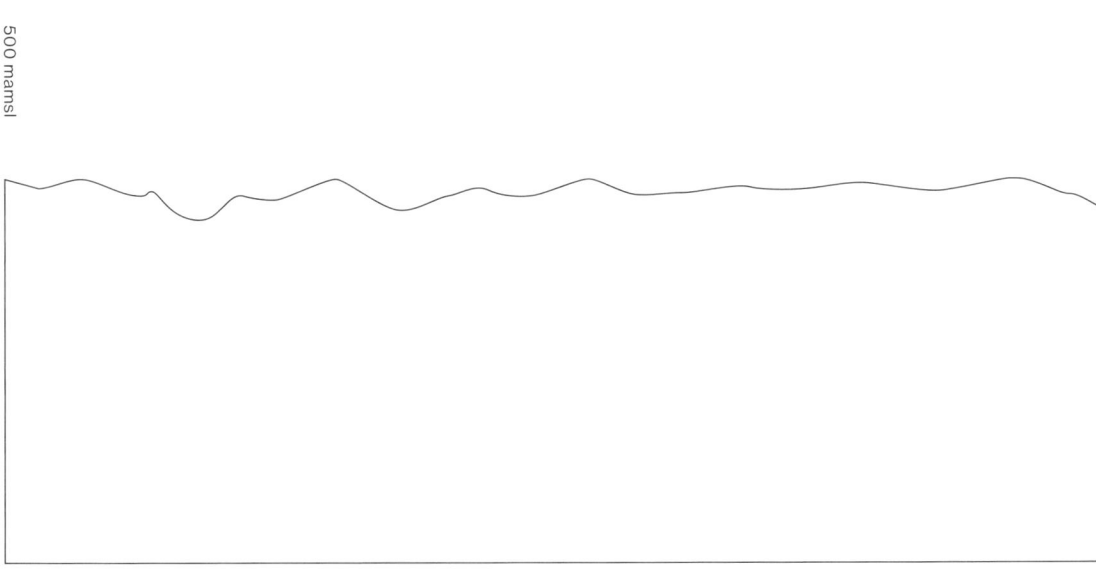

"At the beginning of my walk I am completely with myself. As I walk, I become aware of my physical and mental state. I am all by myself. I feel all the parts of my body. I feel my strength at the first ascent of the path. Reaching the top, my eyes are wide open. The city looks dwarf-ish in the distance and the plain stretches in front of me. I let my thoughts roam freely. The past blends with the moment, and I imagine the future in scenarios. My thought circles cover the landscape. Space and time stand still. There is fog above the lake I am passing. In the meantime, the large oak has lost most of its leaves. A pleasant anticipation catches me every time I pass the first one of our meeting points. Will you appear on the horizon anytime soon? Maybe behind the little forest area? The closer I get to your starting point, the more my thoughts change their orientation and are directed towards you. How are you today? You approach me. I walk towards you, just how I am today, with what I am today."

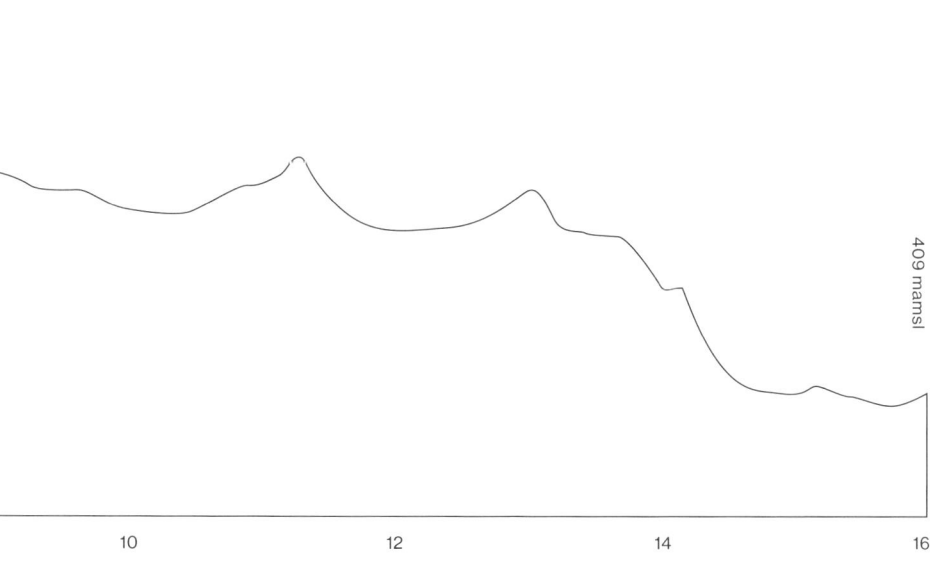

For two decades, we have been developing our work together with Zündwerk at the junction point of art and social systems. At the beginning of our work process, there is usually an observation or an aspect of everyday life, an elusive moment, that draws our attention and stimulates our thoughts. We want to get to the bottom of that matter. Anywhere, at the table, in the studio, or while walking, we wrestle with something that is not yet tangible until we have found words or images for it. It is through the exchange our perspectives that something unique and unexpectedly new emerges. We shift and question patterns of perception and thereby focus on our own perceptive processes. We are interested in the moment of ignition, the initiation of a process, for every sensual perception that is perceived and reflected leads to cognition. The moment of cognition acknowledges the endurance of uncertainty. Our actions usually need little material and are apparently simple; but: "Simple is not just simple. You have to capture simplicity first!", as theater producer Barbara Schlumpf described our work.

Through repetition, approaching each other has acquired a deeper sense and has become the subject of our artistic work for half a year. We are engaged in a somewhat purposeless activity from which no visible workpiece emerges. The emptying of a demand for performance in the activity of walking towards each other and the time that is spent on this path has become an essential part of our week. A way of stepping out of the daily routine, a meandering of thoughts just as the body moves through the topography of the landscape.

By walking towards each other, however, our focus is consciously expanded by one dimension, to that which is most likely to arrive, the meeting. The purpose and aspiration is the actual meeting and time culminates into this encounter. While walking, our focus is not on an orientation in the landscape. Rather, the focus is on moving through space. From me to you. Always along the same line, the same path. The uncertainty in walking towards each other is paired with the certainty of knowing the way. And through that: Being able to step out, to depart from everyday life, concentrating completely on one's own rhythm, on one's own body. The body is actively involved. It bears the immediate perceptions, which become apparent through the recognition of slight changes in the landscape and the awareness of one's own condition. Body, perception, thoughts, and space meet. An embodied encounter with the world. Through the repetition, the continuation of walking towards each other, we have experienced how one's self repeatedly enters into a relationship with the other. The self is the perceived sensations on the way; the other is the landscape, the path or the weather that we encounter as an influential – even resistive – partaker, and the other person. When we meet at one point, both of us are charged with the memories of the individually experienced sensory activity of walking. We relate to each other by walking toward each other – again and again. This marks the impossibility to circulate isolated thoughts; rather it enables us to think/feel dynamically forward – toward the other.

Eva Clara Tenzler
Gehen – Ein Längsschnitt
Walking – Dissecting

Translation by Shannon Sullivan
Walking as Physical Poetry

This text is an invitation to take the sensation of the words as impulse for (the experimentation with) the physical experience of walking or movement.

Schlingend gähnt sich Furche um Weg, leuchtend im Nichts und verborgen in dem Rest, der verweilt. Ein Schritt, der sich vorwärts will. Ein Fußende, das zum Neuanfang wird: Längenmaß einer Zeit.

Gezähltes bricht sich entgegen der Bewegung: Wer beobachtet, geht schon nicht mehr. Wann aber wird es doch wieder zu dem sanften Fließen, das so eigentlich aus dem ersten Atmen kommt. Es ist das Bewegte, das nicht abbricht und pochend drängt. Und da ist sie, die erste Unterbrechung, das erste Halten, Fingerzeig einer Ahnung. *Du streichst empor, verirrst Dich im Tritt, und wähnst nur noch den Kontakt zum Boden. Ein Unten will rufen, eine Waagerechte andeuten, sicher sein. Doch da sinkt es im Senkrechten, ist Schaukeln ins Vorn.* Eine fußläufige Bewegung also, ein Druckpunkt, Austarieren der Vielheit. Ich gebe Gewicht ab in ein Räkeln, das aus den Fasern des Morgens widerhallt. Sich ausdrehend liefere ich mir selbst das Initial, das kantig verharrt und widerständig seiner Gestalt nachgeht. Sachgerecht, formlos, verbindlich.

Bildhaft verzerrt sich ein Wesenszug in der Bewegung, die dem Moment entweicht. Windgleich, wärmer noch, zieht etwas dem Kern entgegen und krümmt ein letztes Mal das Haupt. Endend fahre ich das Du meiner Kanten entlang und verirre mich im Tanz, der meinen Fingern entspringt. Kein Schritt im Gehen, kein Fortkommen. Wiederkehr bahnt sich selbst. So löst sich ein Schwingen von Oben her, ein sanftes Schaukeln in den Ähren, die gestern noch geschlossen waren: Wachsen, um zu verblühen. Ein strebsames Reifen aus dem spiralförmigen Ganzen spricht leis, wenn es ahnt. Und erst das Verlangen gibt schließlich Form in der Dehnung des Verwachsenen. Ein Mehr, das schon veranlagt ist.

Dem Austritt bleibt keine Richtung, wenn er morgens warnend mit dem Nebel entgleist. Sphärischer Dunst nur noch, da verhallt das Rufen und bettet die strengen Worte ein in das Netz aus Wassertropfen, die sich an dem kalten Stein von gestern kondensieren. Ein Schritt nun. Trittflächen auslotend leuchtet der Impuls durch den sehnigen Zusammenhalt. Das Webschiffchen in der Hand fahre ich durch die Stränge hindurch und sinne dem Rhythmus nach. Es festigt sich die Netzstruktur einer Bewegung in der leuchtenden Faltung zur Kenntlichkeit hin. Es gibt kein Verklingen – nur ein Tönen ists, das der Stille eigentlich ist. *Das organische Zusammenziehen drängt sich seinem eigenen Grenzpunkt entgegen, um Wendung und Atmen zu durchdringen, wenn die Schwingung bricht.* Organisierendes und entropisches Wechselspiel im Ganzen wirkt sich so an der Reibungskraft des Bewegten: ein bloßes Organigramm wesenhafter Versuchsanordnungen.

Als Verwandtschaftssystem wird meine Außenform kundig in der sich stetig erneuernden Verbindungslinie aus Kontakt und Impuls, die abstoßend verhältnishaft zueinander Bezug nehmen. Der Boden als ewiger Partner meiner somatischen Umrisse bleibt selbst in Veränderung begriffen und wird Landungszone verdichteter Massenverhältnisse. Er ist Aufnahme, Ausrichtung und Leitbild als Gründungsform des Senkrechten. Ein Kreisel selbst, mich austarierend, schwanke ich der Mitte zu, winde mich empor zu dem seismographischen Pendeln, das sich nur in der Bewegung selbst vertraut macht. Das Berührungsmoment als Sensation; Sinnesvereinigung des Gewordenen in ihrer Erwartung des Kommenden, Hoffnung auf ein wachsendes Weiter, das nicht endet. So also entlastet die Fußsohle sich schließlich auf dem ruhenden Letzten, vollführt die einrollende Bewegung, die dem Gewölbebogen ursprünglich ist. Der Aufrichtung als Endpunkt einer Verhältnishaftigkeit

That which is counted breaks against the movement. Who observes is no longer walking.

You streak upwards, get lost in the steps, only imagine contact with the ground. Below is calling out to you, an indication of a horizontal line, of being safe. Sinking into the vertical. An oscillation forwards.

Organic contraction compacts, saturates, permeates. Twisting and breathing. The vibration cracks.

geltend widerklingt der Richtungsimpuls im sensorischen Raum. Ein weiteres Intervall klanglicher Anordnungen, das sich als improvisatorische Folge ereignet. Und währenddessen der ewige Wunsch, eine Notation zu vollführen, Wiederholbarkeiten zu definieren; Anmaßungen an das Maßvolle.

Als Stoff wallt sich die Ahnung eines Kontaktes durch die Geschichtlichkeit der Linie, die hinter mir liegt. Kahn im Meer, ein sich verendendes Kielwasser, das den Weg beschreibt. *Ich spüre mich anbranden und erneut verformen, nie Form gewesen, immer im Rand geboren als sich entgrenzendes Summen.* Die Atemkehre wirbelt sich als Rückschau in das Wasser hinein und waltet rhythmisch ihrer Wiederkunft. Und doch, da wird etwas Zukunft, will Lesbarkeit nach Hinten weg, birgt sich sein Jetzt. Und weiter bleibt nur der Kontaktpunkt eines wartenden Gegenstandes, der sich Ich heißt. Gegenwart also, stehend und gleißend in dem Absoluten, das ihr innig ist: ein flüchtiges Wesen, Kommen und Vergehen im selben Grunde. Serpentinenhaft entgegen der Steigung wächst ein Weg empor. Eine knorrige Erzählung der Dinge, die einmal waren und die sich nur langsam schleifen. Dem Wind preisgegeben verwindet der Berghang die Schrittfolge entlang seines Lots, das in seiner Mitte pendelnd dem Kommenden zuruft. Schicht um Schicht schält die Wiese ihre Oberfläche in das Geröll hinein, dem Berg gänzlich entblättert. *Mit dem Übertritt verstummt der menschliche Abdruck und waltet wabernd in die weite Stille.* Ich spreche leise, wenn das Gestein einzeln bleibt. Ich senke mich hinein in die kühlende Masse und berühre das Bewegte in mir, das dankt. Eine Demut, die der Weite mitfließt, und mich im Tag vorüberträgt: *Preisgegeben der eigenen Größe, ins Verhältnis gesetzt und berührbar von Licht und Wehen.*

Als Muster zerfällt von Oben die Kluft und vergisst meiner Bewegung. Eingängig, als Leitbild eines Beginns. *Ich pflücke mich selbst in der Spur, die ich aus den Kieseln auflese und beiseiteschiebe.* Dem Wetter hingegeben schwankt nur der Atem noch, wenn er weiterzieht. Schritthaft lenkt mich die Ruhe, die dem Gang inniglich ist. Wiederkehrend, routiniert, ausbrechend. Die Weite kratzt an meiner wundenden Hautgrenze empor, wird drängendes Gegenüber. Ergeben lehnt sich etwas an in mir, birgt sich in das Gelassene. *Einem gespaltenen Holz gleich fasert die Struktur offen und verläuft in ihrem Längsschnitt. Eine ewige Linie, die abreißt.* Ich spüre mich einverstanden vergehen, einer Herde gleich: Ein Kontaktnetz aus fernen Bildern, die mir buchstabiert werden und an meiner Außenlinie ihren Wendepunkt finden. Im Gemeinsamen getrieben, ewig zum Ankerpunkt verloren, und schließlich ein Aufwachen, das aus einem Kältereiz erwächst. Im verholzten Wesenszug, der sich seiner Weite erinnert, streiche ich bedächtig über das leise Ende. Eindimensionalität aller Ebenen, ein wankender Halm in weiter Flur. Hier wähnt keines der Gedankenlieder mehr einen Ton zu vollenden, der gestern noch auf den Lippen lag, und verklingend nur gerinnt die Melodie mit dem Antlitz, das ich vergessen werde. Es bleibt eine wolkenverhangene Regung, die aus einer langen Falte emporschießt und sich selbst in die Kälte blößt. Und schließlich rührt sich etwas.

In dieser Nische schimmert ein Vergessen empor, das rau an meiner Wange entlangschürft. Verborgenes Reißen einer Linie und zählend bis zum Letzten. Das Summen nun wieder, innen liegend und kein Anfang mehr. Es surrt in einem Zwischen rindengleich dem Jetzt entgegen, tastet und prüft. Antwortet. Vielstimmig tönt es in einer polyphonen Mär, die sich nach außen wirkt. Gesträubt und leise entwirrt klopft es seinen ewigen Zyklus. Dem Labyrinth der Hautstrukturen entgleist verwahre ich den Atem des Neuen in der Erinnerung.

I feel myself ebbing and flowing, deforming once again. I was never form. Emerging on the edge, a dissolving hum.

Crossing over the human footprint falls mute, wafts into the vast silence.

Exposed, put into relation. Surrendering to light and air.

I gather myself in the trail that I glean from the pebbles and push aside.

Like split wood the structure discloses fibers running longitudinally. An eternal line that tears.

Fortbewegt, orthaft und entlassen: kenntlich im Jetzt. Abschied nehmend weilt das Dunkel seinem Ausgang. Wachsende Fasern treiben sich noch.

Ein Weg, gegangen aus seinem Ursprung, verlässt lautlos seine Spur. Eine gewundene Strecke des Erzählten walkt neu gestützt in das brandende Geröll hinein. Mein Pfad führt mich durch das Gewachsene, reiht mich ein in das Band, das sich selbst zu weben vermag. Sich abwechselnde Farbspiele entzweien sich auf ein erneutes Wandeln hin und begleiten die Schritte, die ich zäh aus der Masse emporschreite. Verwandt singen sie mir federngleich ihre steinerne Antwort. Bloß verhältnishaft neige ich den Kopf, ziehe meinen Schatten über mich hinweg. Geschält strebt der rohe Kern dem Grat entgegen. *Und hier nun wird es still.* Die Wiesen grünen sich die Hänge hinauf, und dem letzten Baum bläut der Himmel seine Weite. Schale an Schale reiben wir uns in der Zeit. Sandige Fingerkuppen, grau geworden und mit verhärteten Enden, tasten aneinander als grenzende Linien des Einschnitts, der uns birgt, verschlingt und wieder preisgibt. Längst ist der Einschlag des Rhythmischen wiedergekäut. Erneut das Summen. Es dringt aus dem Schritt heraus und windet sich, bevor es in sein Pendeln übergeht. Ein Beginn, streckendes Weiten und Aufbruch, verdächtig einer ewigen Ausdehnung in der schwingenden Folge. Doch nun der Einhalt, die Vibration einer Atemlosigkeit und ein schaukelndes Wider, das regungslos seinen Umkehrpunkt kenntlich macht. Ein Antwortspiel als verwandte Vermessung unserer Distanz: Ein Anstieg nur.

A path, carved from its origin, soundlessly leaves its tracks.

Silence envelops.